LITTLE DIVA ON WHEELS

Little Diva On Wheels

All rights reserved
Copyright 2018 Jennifer Kuhns

The author has made every effort to contact and acquire permission from all persons referenced or mentioned in this autobiography.

Reproduction in any manner, in whole or part, in English or any other languages, or otherwise without the written permission of publisher is prohibited.

For information contact: Shalako Press
P.O. Box 371, Oakdale, CA 95361-0371
http://www.shalakopress.com

ISBN: 978-0-9990070-4-4

Cover Design: Jennifer Kuhns and Nathan Pierce
Cover art and Photographs: Jennifer Kuhns
Formatting by Karen Borrelli
Editor: Staycc Baptista

PRINTED IN THE UNITED STATES OF AMERICA

Dedication

To my family and friends who helped me live my life. Those who accepted me as I am, who supported me in whatever I chose to try, to do, and defended my right to do so.

Little Diva on Wheels

February 18, 1980, held a monumental moment for my parents. It was not only that, but also the beginning of my very own story. It was when I came into the world at 3:14 a.m. As all good stories start, it was a cold, windy, and rainy night. Okay, now that that is out of the way, but I'm told it really was a cold, windy, and rainy night.

I need to share that my story actually started before it should have. I shouldn't have been born until around the end of April or the first of May, sometime after my aunt's wedding. My mom was her maid or maiden of honor (I don't know which is the proper term if she was already married...or maybe it's matron) anyway, because of my early arrival, major alterations had to be made to my mom's dress. I actually don't know what the big deal was because the dress had to be made smaller and smaller is always a good thing, right?

I realize I'm a little off topic here, but you will find I tend to do that...a lot, so consider yourself warned. I'm not big on linear thinking. I lean towards how about, what ifs, let's try, and wouldn't it be cool...and that isn't just my thought process. It is kind of how my family and I have always approached my life in general. If that doesn't work, let's try something else.

So where was I? Born too early...that's where I was headed. Being born ten weeks early put a huge hitch in my get-along, literally. First of all, I weighed three pounds twelve ounces and I had to weigh five pounds before I could even leave the hospital. Not to mention, I couldn't breathe by myself, eat by myself, had to be under bilirubin lights because I became jaundiced. On top of that I didn't have a stitch to wear because, hey, at three pounds twelve ounces, nothing fits. I take that back. There is such a thing as "preemie" diapers and "preemie" knit kimono shirts. Like, seriously?!?!?! I get the diapers, but knit kimono, tie at the side, with dull, bland, pink edging, and a quarter inch ribbon tie? Who decided that was any kind of cute! What kind of style is that? Okay, maybe they sound cute, but in my opinion, looking back at them now, they were far from cute. Anyway, when I was finally able to go home, my grandmother brought over an arm full of doll nightgowns she had made. You know, those little nightgowns sewn up on the bottom so they look like sacks. I'm told I had one called "The Van Gough Bow" that my dad apparently put on me whenever it was clean. I'm guessing it had something to do with a big bow.

Then my grandma started on dresses. Still doll size, but I tell you what, she had some fierce fashion sense. Finally, I was wearing some designer, one-of-a-kind outfits when I was out and about in public. The rest of the time, the hanging at home time, the nightgowns were still my go to wardrobe. You know, like sweats or yoga pants of today, those comfy clothes.

It is my understanding that I was able to leave the hospital five weeks after I was born.

That's when I could breath, made weight, ate without being gavage-fed, and lost the yellow tint to my skin. All seemed to be well with the world until my parents figured out who was really in charge of time, life and how it was going to flow...or not. You see, they didn't really understand the neo-natal life at the hospital; that time has no meaning, lights are always on, music is always playing, people are always singing and poking at you, and you get fed every three hours...around the clock. That's neo-natal life. There is no distinction between night and day. You are awake when you want to be awake, asleep when you want to be asleep, and have your every need met any time of the non-differentiated day or night. That was my first job and my first order of business. My new, first time parents needed to learn how things were going to roll.

    They actually took to it pretty quickly. I ate every three hours, around the clock, just as my parents were told I needed before we left the hospital. It was imperative that I had that constant nourishment because of my less than stellar start in life. I had it on good authority that my mother had a rough go of the every-three-hours thing. As I mentioned before, "non-differentiated day or night", well, it seemed to be an issue for her. The way she explained it to me some years later was that it took her an hour to feed me and then an hour to get me to go back to sleep, which gave her an hour to sleep before the whole process started over again.

    I guess the biggest problem was that it sort of took longer than my allotted two hours to feed me and get me back to sleep, so she spent the first couple of weeks spending her "shortened" sleeping hour not sleeping, but doing chores, working on my baby book, or just sitting in a rocking chair trying to stay awake. Mostly because, I suppose, I had decided not to sleep at all. So, with all that not sleeping at night, my non-differentiated day and night became differentiated, but backwards. All I wanted to do was sleep during the day and be entertained all night.

Apparently, after a couple of weeks my parents decided they weren't fans of my inverted twenty-four-hour clock and reinforcements from Illinois were brought in in the form of my great-grandmother, Mildred Parr. That extra person, that extra pair of hands, as my mom called her, was exhausting! That woman, who incidentally couldn't say my name and called me Jeffner for the week she was visiting, and the rest of her life, didn't have the slightest inclination or courtesy to follow my self-imposed schedule. In fact, that woman, who I have to say I became very fond of when I got older, played, and poked, and annoyed me all day long for days on end, until yes, until one night I was so worn out I actually ate and fell asleep when I was theoretically supposed too. Again, it is my understanding, since I don't actually remember those first weeks and months of my life that some celebrating went on that night, not to mention...dare it be said, SLEEP by all.

And that's how much of the next eleven months went. Me setting a precedent and my parents vetoing that action and implementing another they seemed to prefer.

I'm assuming you caught the eleven month timeline. Odd choice, you might think, but in actuality that is when the reality of having a premature baby presented itself in full force for my whole family.

To back track a bit, my parents had many conversations with doctors and nurses in the intensive care pediatric unit. One such conversation, a curiosity mostly, was why babies were born too early. The answer was a non-answer. The doctor's answer was, "Hey, we don't really know how conception even works or why nine months is the magic number. We have no idea why some babies come early." Not terribly comforting for my parents, but the truth nonetheless, which they appreciated.

Another probably more important conversation was about development. The physical, mental, motor, verbal, and so forth. It was explained that all of my development would be almost three months behind schedule, ten weeks to be more exact, not that babies progress at the same speed anyway, but that gave my parents a starting point. Because I was born ten weeks early, it was explained, my development would be behind by that amount of time.

And remember me saying I couldn't breathe by myself? I suppose you would call that another developmental issue. Oxygen, a key factor in living, would you believe, can and does cause negative consequences or effects if too much is administered. Let me explain. Although we all know oxygen is a needed and "good thing", it can also be detrimental, disadvantageous, and injurious, as with my case, to premature babies.

Oxygen is administered, sometimes in large quantities, to premature babies with heart or lung problems who may need assistance in breathing to get normal levels of oxygen in their blood. The down side to this "Extra Helping" of oxygen can and does cause something called OXYGEN TOXICITY. I don't want to get all medically technical and boring but, for example, a response to too much oxygen or a higher concentration of oxygen I guess, (you see we only need something like 21% concentration and hospitals can deliver a full 100% concentration of pure oxygen) in preemie babies is something called Retinopathy of Prematurity...ROP for short. Okay, that's the technical term. What it means is too much oxygen can cause things like enlarged and/or twisted blood vessels in the eye, detached retina, or even blindness. Of course, there are varying degrees or stages of ROP. They're listed as I, II, III, IV, and V, if you are interested.

  I don't actually know what my stage is, but I have something called transient myopia, or esotropia. What does that mean? Well, it means that I am near-sighted and when I'm tired...or when some well-meaning ding-dong thinks they have to get right up in my face to talk to me, my eyes cross. Oh yeah, and I wear glasses. And of course, as a budding fashionista, several of my first pairs were pink.

  But what was even more devastating to my parents than the possibility of having a blind child was the attitude and flippant response the ophthalmologist gave them at my very first eye appointment. When asked about the concerns of me getting too much oxygen and the possible prognosis of blindness, the doctor's response was less than padded with warm heartfelt concerned condolences, and totally filled with "it sucks to be you."

Back to the eleven-month time line, or should I say the bombshell. As I said earlier, it was explained to my parents, family, and friends that because of my pre-mature birth, I would continually be about three months behind in my development...physical development anyway, as my mental development wouldn't be assessable for some months yet. So, they had absolutely no worries, questions, or misunderstandings about where I was developmentally until my eleven-month check-up. I mean, for God's sake, they were first time parents, with a baby born too early and like zero knowledge of what should or should not be happening, and at what pace. All my parents could do was depend on the professionals, primarily the doctors, to keep them informed about my progression and development.

It was at that appointment, that eleven-month well baby check that the floor was blown from beneath my parent's feet. It was at that seemingly routine appointment that they were told that I was in fact, not developing as expected. That wasn't the shattering news. It was a set-back, yes, probably, but one that just needed time for maturity and mobility. Basically all things related to my body and physicality just needed to catch up to my chronological age.

The bomb that was dropped on my parents was that the "catch up thing" wasn't actually going to happen. It seemed at some point, just before my eleven-month check-up, I had stopped developing in certain areas, actually, kind of most areas, as I understand it. You know, those little quirky, endearing, personality traits one tends to develop as soon as they are born. The way one moves, holds his or her head, sits, eats, plays or even looks at their adoring parents. All those little things, those seemingly naturally occurring, on one's own timeline, developmental stepping stone and bench mark things, that in a cluster don't develop, present a larger and devastating medical condition called Cerebral Palsy.

What's Cerebral Palsy? It is so many things; it's shock, it's devastation, it's heartbreak, it's <u>why is my child broken</u>, and possibly the biggest is guilt. Of all the questions asked, probably the most impactful is, did I/we do anything or fail to do something that caused or contributed to my child's condition...her problem.

I know what you are thinking right now....What actually causes Cerebral Palsy? Ok, again, technically, in my case, it is a brain injury due to lack of oxygen just before, during or after birth. Of course, every case of Cerebral Palsy is unique to each person. And that is because, well, because of many things; type and cause of the damage to the brain, when, why, and how it happened. There is a list longer than both my arms as to the causes. The best answer my parents ever got was from one of my doctors. He said, "We don't really know how conception even works and why nine months is the magic number, let alone why babies are born early and why some of those babies are fine and others are not." Yes, I am repeating something I said earlier, with a little added at the end. The point I'm trying to make is that the practice of medicine may be scientifically based, but medicine has nowhere near the exactness of a scientific formula or equation, especially when applied to life and living things. There are plainly way too many variables.

I feel like I have opened a door for you here and not fully let you in. I feel like I need to, not list, but explain in more detail what Cerebral Palsy is, what it actually affects, the effects of Cerebral Palsy. If you aren't at all interested or don't feel the need to know, feel free to skip this part. To tell you the truth, I've heard it and talked about it all my life and find the topic more than somewhat boring. I am a spastic quadriplegic (bilateral spastic hemiparesis in actual medical lingo) and I do what I do within my capability without reference to or because of my disability.

So, here goes. Cerebral Palsy ranges in severity depending upon the degree of injury to the brain. The effect, the primary effect of CP, (from here on out Cerebral Palsy will be referred to as CP) is the impairment of muscle tone, gross and fine motor function, balance, control, reflex, coordination, as well as oral functions such as swallowing, eating, and speech, all of which, lucky me, I possess. There are some secondary conditions such as sensory impairment, seizures, and learning disabilities. I don't have any of the secondary conditions, except maybe for a learning disability when it comes to math, but I don't think that counts. I'm pretty sure I just hate math and that's why I majored in all things English, Literature, and Writing. So, that's it, CP in a nutshell. If you are interested in a more in-depth explanation, there are a multitude of websites or other resources available to glean information on or about "everything you ever wanted to know about CP."

So, at eleven months all things changed. My parents had to move from an expected "normal" to a new and altered normal. It was less about what was normal and more about what was possible. More specifically, how and what do they do to make as many things possible, possible. My parents' recall is a little understandably blurry for several months after my diagnosis. There were second, and third opinions. There were tests and evaluations. There was my parents' coming to grips with the reality of having a less than perfect child, and then having to share that news with family and friends...then dealing with the "Oh, poor you" comments. My mom and dad also learned in those early days about family love and support, beginning with my Great Uncle Bernard, who happened to be visiting from Iowa at the time of my eleven-month appointment.

You see, Uncle Bernard, my dad's uncle, had his share of heartbreak in his life, as well. His youngest daughter was born with Down Syndrome. Uncle Bernard was not the type of man to sit on his hands or throw them up in the air. He was a doer, a giver, a rock of a man, a "tell me what I can do to support you" kind of man. As one of the founding fathers of Camp Courageous, he always had the best advice. "You'll be fine." And they/we, were/are, fine... as the new normal became part of our lives.

The beginning of that new normal was the physical and mental evaluations conducted by specialists of all kinds, including the brain-wave guy that hooked my head up to some crazy machine with a bazillion wires to determine, what, if any, part of my brain actually functioned as it was supposed to. It was not a fashion look I appreciated and my screams let everyone in the room know my feelings on the subject. My folks teased me years after about Weezy being the only thing that comforted me and eased my anxiety at all. Weezy was known by everyone else as Helen Louise, the name of my other grandmother, my dad's mom, who gave me the doll for my first Christmas. And as medical personnel usually do with pediatric patients, they included Weezy in the testing procedure and had her hooked up as well. Through the test, I hugged Weezy like her life and mine depended on it. Even in that stressful situation, my mom said that watching the Weezy scene play out brought out a little comic relief for everyone. And that is why I blame my parents for my, I don't know, my weird, warped, sometimes inappropriate, *lighten the mood* sense of humor.

    The next step to normal was all about the therapy which also was prefaced with evaluations of my mental acuity and physical mobility. Of course getting set up with the first appointments took several weeks, but when Judy, the head Elks and my first physical therapist, came to the house to see what she had to work with, she told my mom, "She's got smarts beyond her age." I guess when asked what a chicken was, I not only told her it was a chicken, but also explained that chickens laid eggs. Then I proceeded to share the fact that the cow she showed me a picture of was where milk came from.

    Once the evaluations were complete, Judy began showing up at my house once a week to sometimes work and sometimes play. Well, I guess it was really all work, but she was able to make it all fun, or at least trick me into thinking it was all fun. Judy's primary job as a physical therapist was to promote mobility, function and quality of life, and prevent loss of mobility before it happens. What did that mean for me? It meant sitting and bouncing on big blue balls while trying to keep my balance. I had and still have zero concept of balance. My mother has always explained the concept of my lack of balance and equilibrium as such; "When she lies on her back, even flat on the floor, she feels like she is going to fall off the face of the earth."

It meant hamstring stretching. It meant sitting on the floor in crisscross applesauce fashion with Judy pulling my hands to the floor trying to get me to hold myself up. It meant lying on the floor, not really trying to learn to crawl, but how to convince my brain to move one hand in front of the other at the same time I moved one leg in front of the other. Wow, when you actually write it down on paper it sounds kind of confusing, doesn't it? But a brain with full function has no problem multi-tasking and getting the movements conquered in a timely manner….say six months or so. It meant learning to clap, to give a high five, to stand with support and put one foot in front of another, and sitting in my first wheelchair with the tray looking at a cardboard book and turning the pages. All those little, simple accomplishments babies and toddlers make without much fanfare. All those thing I never quite mastered and am still working on at age thirty-eight. I know, why try, right? You try because you have to and because you never know what might be accomplished. If you stop or never try, nothing will ever be accomplished.

And that is kind of where Paula, my first occupational therapist came in. An occupational therapist or OT works on everyday activities, daily living activities, and/or everyday functions. For children occupational therapy covers fine motor movements. Things like eating, brushing teeth, washing hands, and small movement playing; stacking blocks, grabbing cheerios or Jell-O squares and getting them to the mouth, coloring, painting...lots of textural elements, oh and blowing bubbles. (Funny story to follow.)

I have to fess up that I never totally or efficiently mastered any of the "daily living activities." At some point in time, a conversation was had between Paula and my parents about "What really matters to YOU" concerning some of the "functions" she and I were working on. Most specifically, eating and feeding myself. I mean, I could do it, feed myself with a spoon, as long as I had all day and six times more food on my plate than I needed because most of it ended up on the floor, in my hair or the front of my outfit. Talk about non-diva like moments. In other words, my parents had to decide what was really most important to them and to me. Was it more important to feed myself and make a big fat mess just to be able to say I did it myself and chalk it up as an accomplishment, or be fed and be less of an optical sensation, a public spectacle, laced with frustration and embarrassment? My parents, being the let's give it a try kind of people that they were, and still are, took the middle of the road approach. When at home, I fed myself for hours at a time making the biggest mess ever. They pretty much considered it an exercise in fine and gross motor mobility as well as mid-line accessibility. Actual nourishment wasn't the goal.

I remember hearing a story about me feeding myself a popsicle. My grandmother, my mom's mom, the one that made all my one of a kind outfits, didn't quite understand the reasoning behind me feeding myself the drippy, sticky, messy popsicle. She kept trying to take it from me to help me, to feed me. I say try because, first of all, it was mine and she wasn't going to pry it out of my cold and sticky hand if I could help it. Secondly, my mother stopped her by saying, "Leave her be." The conversation that followed was a typical one that took place time and time again over the years.

Grandma: But she is making a mess.
Mom: So, I'll clean her up when she is done.
Grandma: But she is going to drop half of it.
Mom: So, I'll give her another one.
Grandma: But she has to try so hard.
Mom: And that's a bad thing?
Grandma: Well, you're just mean!
Mom: If that's how you see it, don't watch.

All those conversations were in the privacy of our own home where I did play at feeding myself. When we were out in public, to restaurants and such, and family gatherings, my mom fed me; actually she still does. She always said it was a choice between the mental and physical. In other words, I could continually embarrass myself by trying to hold and operate eating utensils, making a disgusting mess and less than appealing exhibit of my physical disability or be judged as a somewhat socially acceptable entity with above average manners; something my mother was always extremely adamant about me having. She once told me, "People are already looking at and judging you as something different and less than human. You must at least have manners to show them different, to show them they are wrong."

The third leg of my tripod of therapy was GOOD OLE GEORGIA BROWN, my speech therapist. Speech therapy addresses several components, depending on the age and need of the client. One part, the part I needed was referred to as "the mechanics of producing words." These mechanics include things like breathing, volume, fluency, pitch, and articulation. I actually remember Georgia more and more vividly than the other two of my therapists. In my mind she was big and fun and the work we did was not work at all. She filled a room not just with size, but more so with her personality, soul, and joy. And she laughed...a lot! Not at me, but with me because I laughed, too. Come to find out, laughing is an exercise in all those things I needed to achieve and conquer;

control of breathing, volume, fluency, and so forth. Believe this if you will, Georgia gave me candy! Yep, turns out if you stick your tongue out with painstaking intensity to lick a candy cane or to lick your lips after a candy cane has been rubbed all over your lips, you are working on building tongue control, positioning, along with the strengthening of the whole oral, word producing cavity.

Although each therapist worked with me in their area of expertise, sometimes those areas overlapped. I remember hearing, yet one more story, on numerous occasions, about one such overlap, which sent my mom into hysterics. Usually, I saw all my therapists on different days, but on one particular day I saw both Paula, the Occupational therapist, and Georgia Brown, the Speech therapist on the same day. Not only did I see them on the same day, but back to back. Remember me mentioning a funny story to follow? This is it.

10:30 a.m., Paula showed up for my OT appointment. On that day she had a new and exciting exercise for me to try. She gathered what she needed, a cup, milk, chocolate to go into the milk because who doesn't like chocolate and wouldn't work harder for it, and a new-fangled thing I had never seen before...a straw. Once she assembled this new "thing", she sat down in front of me and placed it on the highchair tray along with a dish towel because she knew how I hated to get anything on my outfits (still kind of that way). Paula was going to teach me a new "everyday function." She was going to teach me how to suck from a straw, and teach me she did! A wonderful technique I use now on a daily basis because it is easier and neater that trying to drink directly from a cup or glass.

A short hour later, Georgia Brown showed up with yet another new and exciting activity for me to try....blowing bubbles. Now, step into my mother's shoes for just a second. She had a child under a year old who had difficulty figuring out how to sit up on her own, get her hand to her mouth, God forbid, have the co-ordination to put one hand in front the other in order to crawl. Then, having just minutes in between therapists and having just conquered the ability to suck from a straw, a major accomplishment, by the way, the second therapist wanted her to blow bubbles. Do you see my mom's thought process here?

No? Well, let me explain it in her words. With both of my therapists sitting there all proud and excited about what my partially defunct brain astonishingly comprehended, there was no thought or concern, it seemed, to learning the reverse action only moments later, with soap or whatever bubbles are made of at the other end of a straw. A straw that had just rewarded me with one of a girl's best friends, chocolate milk. Mom's question, "How is this a good idea? You know she is going to suck in bubbles, get sick, and blow nothing but chunks afterwards, right?" At that point, logic set in and the therapist agreed that learning opposite actions or ideas in the same day was probably not the best idea.

So, Georgia Brown switched gears and that day I spoke my first complete sentence--"God damn it dogs, shut up!" This of course, clued my first-time parents into the fact that learning by imitation is definitely a thing. A thing that they needed to be more aware of and clean up a bit. Why that sentence? Well, of course as every middle class American family, we had dogs. The dogs' outside pen and play area was along the side of the house right by the kitchen window where the kitchen table and my highchair sat. Dogs being the animals they are, they barked at every little thing. Hence, the phrase, the sentence I heard countless times during a day was, "God damn it dogs, shut up!", thus proving that repetitive actions, exercises, or play had a result...positive or negative. In this particular instance, positive or negative was debatable depending on the person's point of view. Georgia Brown was pleased as punch and absolutely delighted at my use of a full sentence with proper inflection, tone, volume, and breathe control, no matter the content, or more probably, because of it. And although my mother was a tad shocked and embarrassed, both she and Georgia Brown laughed hysterically, noting that that was absolutely baby book worthy.

  And that is how things went, how I progressed (or not), and how I grasped and attempted to implement the various concepts of everyday living. My days were very similar to the Bill Murray movie, *Groundhog Day,* with repetition of any and every action and movement all day, every day. I vaguely remember one of my go-to everyday activities. It was called "Bucket Time." Bucket Time was when I was propped up in the corner of the couch with a big plastic bucket in-between my legs that was filled with all kinds of things that I stirred, rifled through, and tried to pick up. The things in the bucket changed periodically so it was always a surprise. I now know that it was not only an exercise in balance, mid-line accessibility, fine motor and gross motor development, but it was also an exercise in independent play. Learning to be by myself. I actually secretly believe that it also gave my mom a breather.

Speaking of breathers, my favorite thing to do with my dad usually happened after dinner. Thinking back thirty some odd years now, I'm guessing it was my dad's way of giving my mom what we now call "quite time." Yeah, no...It was really give mom a breather time. Anyway, my dad and I would go downtown and find a bench in front of the Veteran's Hall and sit and observe. Actually, he would sit on the bench. I of course by that time traveled fully accommodated in my own chair. By the time we started doing that, I had my orange chair. It was a combination wheelchair, highchair, car seat that was the most god-awful orange you have ever seen! I mean really, Orange! Let's make the weird, different kid even more obnoxious looking, and draw attention and frame the differences in bright orange. Most likely designed by some, in my opinion, over-educated adult (probably an engineer) who believed using a stand out color like orange was the way to go. If I were to hypothesize now, I would be more inclined to believe that the orange Naugahyde fabric used on those chairs was rejected or unwanted material, un-usable and unacceptable to be used for anything else. I mean really, can you think of the last time you saw a recliner or a luxury car upholstered in orange Naugahyde? Me neither... Anyway, that is absolutely the way to, what I believe all disabled people desire, to be part of the whole, part of the normal, part of the accepted contributing part of society by making them stand out and having less than no fashion sense whatsoever...NOT! I fully believe "they," whomever they were or are, were of the opinion that the children in those God-Awful-Orange chairs didn't have the ability to care one way or another. I may or may not have mentioned this before, but, when adult folks see a kid in a wheelchair they automatically think retarded, deaf, dumb, and blind, and every other negative attribute a person could have.

    On the other hand, children are totally a horse of a different color. After hours and hours of research, as well as personal experiences and observations, in my opinion, kids are the complete opposite of adults. They have no preconceived notions about, well, about anything at all, really. Don't get me wrong. Children are not oblivious to the world around them no matter how much adults, especially parents, try to block it from them. Children live in the same world as adults, see the exact same things, and are affected by the same conditions. The difference is that children, unlike adults, have not had the opportunity to develop any opinions about anything. They have not formed negative opinions or are not prejudiced against those who are different than themselves.

    There are several old sayings that I have heard over the years—*You can't judge a book by its cover, Beauty is only skin deep, Good things come in small packages, People who live in glass houses should not throw stones,* and *You cannot judge a man until you know his whole story*—all of which were told to me by adults. Why bring this up? My point in bringing up these examples is that I have always heard considerable preaching about looking to the inside of a person for wholeness when it is most evident that the physical aspect of a person is what is judged by today's society.

Here I go, getting way off topic again and all opinionated and evil. But you have to understand that it all comes from my experiences and interpretations of those experiences, how other's opinions, actions, responses, or lack thereof, have affected me. I am under the assumption that you picked up this book because you wanted to understand or get an inside perspective on what it is like being physically disabled...how we feel, what we think, how we deal with society and those around us, and how we are treated.

I believe it all begins with the education of children, but I have also come to understand that that can't happen until adults are first enlightened, re-educated, and then re-evaluate what is truly important in life before they impart their values and knowledge on to their children.

Why am I qualified to discuss and make such claims on the subject? Well, first and foremost, I am disabled and have lived the reality of being stereotyped as being less than whole, as well as being prejudged and pitied. I have had my head patted and been told that I am an inspiration, categorized as a waste of time, space and energy, and so forth.

The second qualification I feel I have to discuss and make certain claims is due to my own personal curiosity about the development and implementation of accepted attitudes toward people with disabilities which led to countless hours and the completion of a 114 page research project. If you are at all interested, I have included an excerpt of said research project in the back of this book which includes my own thoughts and reflections on the books and articles reviewed.

Now that my rant is out of the way, this is a perfect time to introduce into my story, Janice, the first shining star, my next door neighbor who is ten years older than me. I met Janice when her family moved in next door to mine when I was about two years old. She was the first person outside of my mom and dad who treated me like a "normal" person, like a regular little kid. Janice taught me how to do things like chew bubble gum without swallowing it. She taught me that a person's heart is as big as their fisted hand. Being twelve years old, Janice was in love with the group Menudo, Rickey Schroder, and the movie *Annie*. So, of course, by default, they became my obsessions, as well. So much so, that Janice would come to my house and ask my mom if I could go to her house for a while, ya know, just like friends do. She'd roll me in my orange chair to her house where, for hours, we would listen to and sing with Menudo, watch *Silver Spoons*, and practice...are you ready, our rendition of the play, *Annie*.

Yes, Janice included me in everything, not only everything she did, but everything the neighborhood kids did. I was the youngest member of "The Garage Club." What pray tell is a Garage Club, you're asking now. Well, it was any garage available on the block where Janice could whip all us kids into a preforming phenomenon, *Annie* being one of those performances. Although, my garage seemed to be preferred because it had a ramp, for obvious reasons, that made for a spectacular prop. Looking back, Janice not only included me, she without pause, used and incorporated what I had to offer as a contributing member of the group. I was never any different. Well, obviously I was different, but not to the neighborhood kids. I was Jenni, the youngest, cute little blonde girl on the block. I was like everyone's little sister that they played with, dressed and protected. And all this is what reinforces my belief that children are not born with preconceived notions about people, or anything, really, but are taught.

I'm sure that is when and where my "diva-ness" was solidified. I am probably the only two or three-year old that wore outfit coordinated leg warmers, Gunny Sax dresses, and fish bone braids influenced by the times and my pre-teen friends.

Of course there were also some un-diva-like times, behavior, or apparel that I recall. The first were the bibs. Ya, bibs...I mean bibs that I wore all the time, not just when I ate. I really don't even want to admit it now, but the truth is, I had a massive problem with containing my saliva within the cavity designated for such things as teeth, tongue, and spit. In other words, I had a massive and continual drooling issue due to the lack of muscle control...or brain connectivity to appropriate swallowing muscle. Therefore, the front of my clothing was always soaked. And that is where the bibs came in. My mom, probably like all moms, was and still is I should add, a very creative person, especially when it came to resolving problems. Staying with the fashion trends of the time, she took decorative handkerchiefs, cut them in half and sewed half a washcloth to the underside which she then tied loosely around my neck calling them "accent dribble rags." I had dozens of those bibs or dribble rags that coordinated with all my outfits. I thought I was gorgeous and styling at the time, and I got to change them several times a day so it was like a new outfit each time. Fast forward a couple of decades and what do you see? Cute, colorful, stylish handkerchiefs around every neck of Every. Dog. In. The. Nation. So much for a two-year-old's style sense and a mother's ability to spin a deficit into a positive.

Speaking of deficits and once again style, let me address the topic you may be wondering about...potty training. Yep, a giant issue for any new mother or father, for that matter. My parents were told that I would probably never be able to control my bladder muscles or bowel movements. Basically it was suggested that instead of being disappointed, they shouldn't bother even trying to potty train me.

Now, let me ask, what parent do you know that would not even try or give their child a chance to succeed? I mean succeed at anything and everything. I'm thinkin' NOT A ONE!

My mom was on the same page as the rest of the parenting world. She was determined to give me the opportunity to at least try and be "normal" in this instance. Okay, maybe in reality she was testing the advice of the medical professionals. They said I couldn't do it. She said, "Okay, let's give it a shot and if it doesn't work, well, we tried." And I, through action, said, "Watch me, watch me!" This "let's give it a shot" approach is how I and my siblings were raised, always.

    I, of course, was not an instant potty prodigy like I'm leading you to believe. There were miscommunications, accidents, not "recognizing the feeling", not wanting to be bothered, all the usual, and dare I say normal, issues that come with potty-training. There were a couple of things that helped tremendously, though. The first was the silky, satiny, big girl panties. For the most part, these super light-weight fabric panties allow the urine to run through them and down a girl's leg, leaving said kid feeling embarrassed, yucky, and waiting for whatever else might or might not happen. I, on the other hand, was in love with my pretty, soft, frilly, fancy, girly big girl panties. When I had an accident in my big girl panties they were swiftly removed and replaced with the ugly, super thick and absorbent, did I say "ugly", white training pants. Do you hear that? They weren't even called panties. They were PANTS. How un-diva-ish….I wasn't having it! Needless to say, I not only was trainable, I excelled with the right motivation.

    Expanding on the use of motivation for potty-training, I explicitly remember making it clear, or as clear as a two-and-a half-year-old could, that I wanted to go to school. How am I connecting the two? Let me explain. Remember the neighborhood kids that I played with every day? Well, one day they were all gone. The street was empty. The garage was empty. And, Janice never came to get me. After having the concept of "school" explained to me, I decided that I wanted to go to school like everyone else. I was especially excited after hearing that I had the prerequisite requirement filled, or close to it, being fully potty-trained. I was told I could go to school if I didn't have any more accidents. Bribery!!!!! That really was not a condition or requirement of special education preschool! But I didn't know that and I worked hard to accomplish that goal. The first of many, I have to say. As a side note, I was one of probably three in the class that were potty-trained. Mothers can be so sneaky...

There were lots of things I didn't know about preschool, or at least the preschool I was going to attend. Although I didn't realize it for some time, like years later, my preschool was a special education preschool that ran in conjunction with the local Head Start program. So, every child in my class had a physical or mental disability. Since my mental capacity was and is totally intact you might be thinking "oh, poor thing." But in reality, I didn't see it that way. I didn't see those kids any different than I saw the neighborhood kids. I can see the question mark on your face...okay, not really, but you know what I mean. Let's see if I can come up with an example.

In class there was a student named Eddie who was blind. Just an FYI at this point, at two and half years old, because of Eddie, I could tell you how to properly set a table. Why? Because Eddie needed the concrete, set in stone, always the same, tactile representation of....kind of everything. In the table setting instance, all of us learned that the glass was at ten o'clock in relation to the plate. On the plate itself the muffin was at two o'clock, the apple sauce was at six o'clock, and so forth....always. If not, then it was on the floor.

In my mind, Eddie was no different than Gloria, the girl who wore super big, fat, ole' glasses from the block. Again, you are probably questioning my comparison. Well, Gloria, who became a medical doctor, had her own need and desire for concrete, set in stone, always the same, in her case, formulaic representations of what she needed to learn and know to become the doctor she strived to be.

As a second example, remember Janice and the garage gang? She and the rest of the group taught me very important unique, what shall we call them...life skills. I learned the words to all the most popular songs. I learned how to chew bubble gum (to the chagrin of my mother) and I learned that my heart was as big as my fist. On the other hand, I learned American Sign Language in preschool because my classmate, Abigail, was deaf. If I wanted to talk to her, I had to speak her language as did we all. And everyone needs to understand when someone says "I have to go to the bathroom!"

Probably the biggest unknown and frightful thing about preschool happened on the very first day. I wasn't aware of it before-hand, but my mom wasn't spending the day there with me. Well, she wasn't intending to spend the day there with me. I, of course, wasn't too cool with that and had my own rendition of how that first (and every other day) was going to go down. And that "is" what did happen that first day and for some time after. Although, towards the end of the second week I did notice she was more often than not in the teacher's office, outside, or in the kitchen helping prepare snacks or lunch. In other words, away from me. And to be honest, I was actually ok with it because I was making new friends and learning all kinds of new things. I also had Sarah, my very first one-on-one aide. I don't remember a lot about her, but I do remember her teaching me jokes. Yes, jokes! Since so many of my classmates had mental disabilities or challenges, and less than (without sounding mean and snarky) pristine brain function or recall, Sarah quickly found out for herself that I was a parrot when it came to hearing, retaining and spouting out whatever information I was fed. Actually to this very day my mom calls me her Human Blackberry. Anyway, Sarah taught me jokes. The one I most remember is "pink, pink, you stink."

    As a side note: Several days ago I was working on the cover for this book and posted a rough draft on Facebook. The picture was as it appears on the cover now. Many people reacted and commented on the cute little girl they remembered. But surprisingly, quite a few remembered the little girl that told the joke...Pink, pink, you stink...and how funny she thought it was.

    But back to my mom. As I became more familiar and comfortable with the new situation and surroundings of my new school and friends, my mom eventually was slowly able to remove herself totally from, not only my sight, but also from the school grounds entirely. Which I'm guessing gave her some more of that "quiet time" my dad and I gave her when he and I sat downtown people-watching. The reinforcing and stabilizing factor to the whole thing was the fact that mom was always there waiting for me at the end of the school day. I never had to wait for her or freak out because she wasn't there. I was never forgotten. I was never in fear of being left. That's how the next couple of years went. Preschool during the morning. Janice and the Garage Gang in the afternoon.

    Speaking of fear of being left, I just had a flashback of the summer of 1982, when my sister was born. I was being babysat by my grandmother and my aunt Karen, alternately, while my dad was at the hospital with my mom. Just to clarify, I was not the one fearful of being left during this time, nor were my grandmother or aunt...really. Each, at different times on separate occasions, locked me inside their cars with the keys in the ignition. I think I just heard you gasp. Not to worry. All things turned out fine.

    Now, the scene that played out in both instances was an absolute true comic relief in my eyes. With panic stricken faces, they both attempted and succeeded I might add, to distracted and occupy me with silly dances, funny faces, and weird noises. I had no clue either time that we were having "an issue." I just thought they were trying to entertain me and have fun. Not so the case as I understood later when the "don't tell your mom about this" line was embedded into my brain.

You have to understand, in 1982, there were no cell phones! Okay, maybe there were huge suitcase size things called car phones, but regular people didn't have them, not like cell phones today. So the dilemma for both my grandmother and aunt was how to get help, not leave me alone, and get the car unlocked, quickly, without freaking me out, or creating too much drama.

By using their "good old country woman ingenuity", both came up with the same solution. I don't recall what either of them used, a rock, a brick, or some kind of hard object, but they both decided to break the window furthest away from where I sat in the car. Did I hear another gasp? At the end of the day all things were as they should be. The kid was safe, happy, and unharmed. The windows were replaced and no one was the wiser. At least not until many, many years later when the story surfaced at a family gathering. I should say stories. The best part wasn't that my mother didn't know what happened, it was that my grandmother didn't know it happened to my aunt, and my aunt was not aware that it happened to my grandmother, only two or three days apart. I still laugh when I think about it. Can I keep a secret, or what?

Anyway, after preschool came kindergarten, with "normal" kids. (Although I have to tell you, I already thought I was a normal kid doing normal kid stuff.) I was mainstreamed at this point into a regular classroom with regular kids for the first time. But prior to being admitted to this "regular school" my mom, my dad, and I had to attend a multitude of meetings. That litany of meetings those of us on the inside called the alphabet soup of objective setting, goal reaching, everybody has to have a finger in the pot meetings, such as IEP, CCS, VMRC, and the list goes on. Presented at one of the first meetings was a letter from my pediatrician, Dr. Stein, M.D., the guy who not only wore black horn-rimmed glasses but also always wore the classiest, most-coolest bow ties...in my opinion...ever! Talk about a guy's fashion statement. He had me from the get-go with polka dots!

    This letter addressed concerns brought up by the Health Services Administration of the Hollister School District. In this letter, Dr. Stein basically gave them a rundown on my medical history, health, and informed them that "Physical abilities and her intelligence and understanding should be the guides to her educational planning." In other words, Dr. Stein was saying that there were no medical concerns or reasons for the school administration to think they could or should limit my ability to attend their regular school, and to base my learning experience on my functioning brain rather than my less than perfectly functioning body. That is when the word "adaptation" was firmly placed into my vocabulary.

    It was also at one of those meetings that I met Peggy, my next one-on-one aide, one that I would have from kindergarten through second grade. I also had the chance to meet my new teacher, Mrs. Farnsworth. Actually, this became a habit for me to meet my teachers a short time prior to school starting. As was usually the case, most teachers had never had a disabled student in their class before me. I was always the first, the guinea pig. It gave us all a chance to get to know one another or become familiar with each other's needs, expectations, and probable classroom strategies...again adaptations.

The funny part about this is the fact that my new schoolmates were only "new" schoolmates once. My teachers were always my new teachers. Each year I had to go through the introductory process again. Each teacher had to be brought up to speed and address the OMG issues that I seem to bring to the surface; the what desk does she use, what restroom does she use, how is she going to do group work, how is she going to keep up...and what seemed to be most important to them was "how do I explain her to the rest of the children?"

That's the funny part. The rest of the children were already up to speed and had no OMG issues with me whatsoever after our first meeting in kindergarten. Actually, when I entered kindergarten the kids, for the most part, especially the boys, were more interested in my wheelchair than me being in it. They were continually pulling, twisting, and tugging on cords and wires, as well as grabbing the control box handle and jamming it forward or backwards. It was like riding a bucking bronco or something. To my mother's credit, once again, she suggested that they take me out of the chair and let my classmates each have a turn at driving the elephant in the room. Had I not already been sitting on the floor watching this hilariously funny activity unfold, I would have fallen to the floor laughing. The classroom walls were never going to be the same again. Thinking back, it might have been fun to have the kids write their names by the holes they made...or not.

After that, we were all part of a whole. I know, kind of an odd statement, all part of a whole. How can that be you might be thinking? Yes, I was an oddity and a big deal when I entered kindergarten, but only then, only once. And only once did Marco, the most outrageous, out spoken kindergartener ever, ask, "Hey, were you born in that chair?" As a matter of fact, more often than not each of my new teachers would get a full rundown of me and what was and was not wrong with me, not from me, but from my very talkative, protective and disability educated classmates.

There was one, small, slight glitch in Dr. Stein's "no medical issues" that might limit my ability to attend their regular school. Six months into my scholastic career I hit a speed bump. During the month of February, the month of my birth if you will remember, I got the worst birthday gift ever! I had known about it for some time, but actually having it done was way worse. Let me give you some background before I tell what I got for my birthday. At this point you have read and know that I had been in a wheelchair for a few years at this point. Yahoo me! One of the youngest children ever to have been put in and able to drive an electric wheelchair, I've been told.

But not all good things come from modern technology. Yes, I could get around my house, my neighborhood my street, my school, and my classroom by myself...mostly, but unbeknownst to me or my parents, and probably my doctor at the time, I had developed bothersome physical and skeletal issues. Because I spent most all my waking hours in the wheelchair, in a sitting position, my right hip had its own rebellion against my anti-bipedal posture.

I won't make you go look that up. I learned that term in college and now at thirty-eight years of age and while writing my story, this book, although I understood it at the time, I sooo fully get it now.

Bipedal means walking up-right on two legs. This position places the ball of the hip into the hip socket which makes it a working joint. The pressure put on that joint from standing and holding your own body weight holds that ball securely in the socket. Because I was always in the seated position, there was not the needed weight bearing pressure to hold the ball in the socket. This allowed the ball to shift and slide out of the socket and consequently stretch tendons and so forth, creating what doctors called a continual partial dislocation.

Why the right leg or only the right leg you might be asking, now. Mostly because I am left-side dominate. That means I am basically left handed. I have more strength and slightly more control on my left side (or as much as a quadriplegic could have). Also because of my spasticity I push down harder on that side, the left side, which does two things. First, it kinda sorta made what was supposed to happen,

happen, push the ball into the socket on the left side, which is a good thing. Secondly, it threw my body all catawampus, which threw my right side totally to the wind...no pressure, no weight, no control, no anything.

Now that that is explained and out of the way, back to my birthday. Around the time of my birthday I was unceremoniously wheeled, not in my wheelchair, but in a hospital bed into the Operating Room to, again, make an adaption, this time to my "being." More specifically, my orthopedic surgeon was going to magically, in my mind, get the ball and hip socket to develop a better bond, a more favorable and normal relationship than they were having. In all honesty, in reality, his plan was to cut and shorten the inside leg tendon so it would hold things in place where they should be. And it worked.

Then came the part that didn't work (enter *Jaws* bad thing are going to happen music)...the part that no one told me about. Yes, the infamous "they" told me I was getting a cast. Yes, they told me it would hurt some and be sore. What they didn't tell me was that I was going to be in a half body cast for what sccmcd like an eternity, six weeks, and I wasn't going to be able to go to school, or at least not "at" school. Those were the long-term issues I had sprung on me. The short term turmoil of my surgery I remember being immediately far more traumatic in my almost six-year-old mind.

First and foremost, I wanted that damn IV thing off, or out, or disconnected, or whatever had to be done to take it away. My mom reminded me during the writing of this story of the ugly discontent which apparently could be seen on my face and heard in my voice. I was adamant about wanting it out. She was adamant that it couldn't come out until I drank some water...something about keeping the IV open until the medical personnel were satisfied that I was not going to throw up or have any other adverse reaction to surgery or medications. I know, eeewwww, right?

The problem was miscommunication. I did not know that A led to B, that drinking water was directly related to the IV being removed. For what seemed like hours, my mom kept forcing the drink water activity in a gentle coaxing manner, with no success. I remained defiant. I didn't want water. I wanted the IV gone and I wasn't going to drink anything until it came out, never to be seen again!

Then my mom finally took the adult route, which I have to say both my parents tended to lean towards when explaining things to all three of us kids growing up. "Look, Jen," she said. "As soon as you drink water and show that it stays down, that you don't get sick or anything, the nurse will pull the IV."

It only took a split second for me to become exceedingly thirsty. I drank. I didn't puke. The IV came out and we moved on to better things, like painting fingernails, making beaded jewelry, activities my totally prepared mom had planned and brought along to the hospital...until I had to pee.

Now, let me ask you, how do you un-teach a socially expected behavior, one punishable if disregarded and ignored? After letting my needs be known and a little hustle and bustle around the hospital room by my mom and a nurse, to my utter shock and horror, they produced a weird looking blue half bowl that they said I was going to .....aaaaa....use. What they meant was that I was not getting up to use the proper facilities, but I was essentially, in my mind, going to pee the bed. I was so not cool with that. Not only did it contradict everything I had ever been taught and scolded for "accidentally" doing, but to intentionally wet the bed was way un-diva like under any condition whatsoever by anyone!

Little did I know that that was going to be the way I was going to go to the bathroom for the next six weeks because of the half body cast I was sent home in. There was one up side though, I could lay in the living-room on my full length body pillow, watch the Disney channel (which my parents got for me for my recovery time), and yes, pee (and the other thing) in the pan, all at the same time without moving, or getting in any kind of trouble. The visual is a little disgusting I know, less than diva-like…eh, maybe, but hey, the issue had to be fixed and a girl's gotta do what a girl's gotta do.

There were times, of course, that I needed to be mobile and in my wheelchair. But with my legs casted completely straight with a brace and stabilization bar attached in between them, well, talk about awkward. My legs had to either be in line with my upper body at 180 degrees, hence the laying down, or at a right angle, 90 degrees to my body, with my casted legs out straight in front of me. There was no bending at the knee possible which created a problem. The day I was released from the hospital my dad brought my wheelchair for me to use on the ride home. The thing looked totally bizarre! He had built a seat extension, a sort of pie-shaped platform that stuck out in front of the existing wheelchair seat. And even though it was stuffed and upholstered in my favorite color, purple, it still looked like some kind of construction vehicle.

That was the first homemade adaptation that I remember. I'm sure there were others before, that I don't recall, but I do know it was one of many, many alterations and modifications made to allow me to be "able", differently, but still "able." I'm betting that was when my dad developed second thoughts about previously teaching me how to "be able" to do wheelies, to the total dismay of my mother. That's probably when wheelie bars were added to the back of my chair to prevent me from flipping over backwards. Not that I ever did flip it over, but I could make my wheelchair jump and buck like a bucking bull.

After family and family friends became accustomed to, accepting of, and comfortable with my condition, my disability, that is how life progressed. They all proceeded through life with a "we'll figure it out" and a Tim Gunn's (way before Tim Gunn, I might add) "make it work" attitude. I had hand braces with crayons and pencils attached so I could draw and...I was going to say write, but I never really got a handle on that. I had a swing that looked like a 1960's Formica kitchen chair with a harness hung by heavy duty chains from a wooden frame so I could play and swing with my siblings. I had a compact industrial keyboard with oversized keys to compensate for my lack of midline accessibility. Which I have to add right here, to this day, not having great midline accessibility really sucks when your nose itches!

But should things not work, should all attempts at a given activity or venture fail, like the page turner that didn't work for **** unless the book was 100 years old with broken binding, I'd be ushered on to the next feat, the next possible accomplishment, envisioning my next attainable goal.

Once again, I took a little side trip, but I thought it was an important detour to share about family, friends, adaptations, the idea of inclusion. Another thing I didn't know beforehand, before having the surgery, as I mentioned earlier, was that I wasn't going to be "attending" school during my six-week recovery time. One more thing sprung on me that I wasn't at all happy about. What I did have was a visiting home school teacher. The funny thing is, although I remember all of the therapists and aides, their names, their families, their birthdays, and so forth, I've had over my lifetime, I have absolutely no recollection of the visiting teacher at all. I don't even remember how often she came or for how long. I suppose she was a nice lady, but again...no recollection...no clue.

What I do remember vividly about that time was being royally pissed off because I was not allowed to go to school and see my friends. Yes, the neighborhood kids visited when they could after school. But it wasn't the same as going to school. The neighborhood kids always came to play with me, cast or not. But without the daily routine of going to school, something that I learned to love from my very first days at preschool, I felt a sense of detachment from something I had been included in and a part of as an intricate part of a whole. Yes, I know. I'm sounding all Holier than Thou, like my attendance was necessary for the entire educational system to function properly. Not what I was going after. Being part of a group, a classroom of kids, being part of something that made me feel like a part of something, being included, treated and thought of as a regular, normal kid was what was missing for me. I felt like a chunk of me was removed. And that being treated as a "normal" kid thing had been removed. The thing is, I thought I was a normal kid and always had!

It was at this point, in my six-year-old mind, that I questioned the inequality, and the reasoning behind my being segregated from my daily scholastic routine. I mean there had been other kids in my class that had had broken arms, legs or this that or the other thing and THEY were still allowed to go to school...daily. What was it about me, my situation that interfered with my ability to attend school? I didn't see a difference between them and me. And to be honest, I don't think most of them did either.

So, as a very verbal and highly vocabulary progressive child, I formulated and presented the question to my mother while I sat and watched her do the dishes one night. I say highly vocabulary progressive because I still hear stories about how I attempted to use one hundred dollar words, quite frequently, incorrectly. As an example, my uncle had his appendix removed at some point and I continually repeated the story with one slight variation as "my Uncle Pete had his Independence out", and then couldn't figure out why every adult in the room laughed.

Another example arose after I had my hip surgery. While explaining to people what had been done and inviting them to view the giant "incision" I continually referred to it as my giant "indecision."

Back to my confrontational question to my mother...Why couldn't I go to school with a cast like everyone else, like the other kids in my class?

She stopped washing dishes and I could see a noticeable "oh crap" look on her face. Actually, I didn't really have a name for that look until many years later, but there was a definite change of expression. She dried her hands and we walked and rolled to the kitchen table.

"Here's the deal, Jen," she began. "You know how you use a wheelchair to get around...all the time and most other people don't? Like even your brother and sister don't use a walker or jumpy seat, or anything anymore?"

"Well, ya ..." I answered like it was a fact of life and no big deal. But it was at that exact moment that I began to understand. "Ya, how come? Why can't I walk like everyone else?" And in that split second, I went from being a "normal kid" to not. I had flashes of doing normal stuff, like eating, bathing, dressing, going to the bathroom, writing, doing my hair, yes...walking, playing, riding a bike, but not actually doing any of it, or at least not by myself. The not going to school with casts on my legs in an adapted wheelchair was a question that was not even on my radar anymore.

"Kiddo," she began. "You have a condition that most everyone else doesn't. You have something called Spastic Quadriplegic Cerebral Palsy."

I remember being very offended by what I interpreted my mother to have said. "I AM NOT A SPAZ!" were the next words out of my mouth, that being a popular term at the time.

"I didn't call you a spaz," she said, "I said you "have something called Spastic Quadriplegic Cerebral Palsy'. There is a big difference between the two."

It was at that moment that a lot of things came together and started to make perfect sense to me. Peggy for example. Peggy wasn't the classroom aide, she was *my one-on-one* aide. At lunch time, Peggy sat next to me and fed me while the other kids fed themselves. When the other kids in my class had to go to the bathroom they just raised their hand and asked Mrs. Farnsworth if they could go, and they went...by themselves. I, on the other hand, had to tell Peggy, she then told Mrs. Farnsworth, and then we went, her and I ...together. That was a real light bulb moment for me! No one else needed assistance to go to the restroom. I'm not talking about getting to the actual facilities, here. I could drive my wheelchair myself. I'm talking about the actual act of "going" to the bathroom. Peggy, as my one-on-one aide, had the (fill in the blank, here...privilege, job, daunting task) of physically lifting me out of my chair and onto the toilet, which involved multiple steps that I won't get into here, but I'm sure you get the picture of what "went down."

The thing is, this was my normal. I not only had Peggy at school, but I had my mom and dad at home performing the same tasks for me. Again, it didn't hit me until the epiphany that my two siblings were also different than me settled in. They fed themselves because they were able to do so. One of the two was able to go to the bathroom by herself without help. My brother was in the end stages of big boy underwear training so I could only assume he too one day would be able to make the trip to the loo alone.

Okay, I'll get back to the spaz discussion with my mom in a minute, but all this talk about bath-rooming reminded me of the biggest and most memorable mistake that I have ever made...to this day! As I mentioned, Peggy was by my side all day every day at school. For some reason, I don't really remember why or what possessed me to do it, but I peed my pants at school...not once but several times without saying a word to anybody. As if that wasn't bad enough, when I got home and the babysitter realized that I had wet myself so much that my hair was soaked with urine as well, she called my mother at work and relayed the story, or should I say the lie, that

I had manufactured. Obviously my brain function was proven to be so totally intact that day because of the detailed recount, the believable rendition of what took place that day that I had my mom believing that the school was at fault. And you know, which I didn't know at the time, when a mama bear believes one of her young has been compromised, she is on it. Taking names and getting facts.

Are you dying to know the story, the contrived lie of a six-year old? Well, today, years later, I have no recollection of why I had multiple accidents, I'll call them, that day. Well, yes I do. I knew peeing my pants was unacceptable. I decided having had one "accident", I couldn't tell Peggy when I needed to go again because I was already wet and I knew I'd be in trouble. My "solution" was to tell her for the rest of the day that I didn't need to go to the restroom and continue to pee myself. This, of course, created another whole issue. How was I going to explain why I came home in the condition I did. I also knew it was unacceptable to lie. And therein lies the problem.

I don't know where it came from, but I came up with doozy of a story even kids much older than I would have been impressed by. The story went:

Peggy was not there at school that day. I had a substitute aide that didn't understand me. Without Peggy, even Mrs. Farnsworth didn't understand me. I tried ALL day to tell someone I had to go to the restroom and no one understood me so I ended up having an accident.

At least that was the story I went with until my mom came home from work, early. Little did I know she had already been to the school, spitting nails, by the way, in hyper-confrontational mode, ready to have someone's job over the lack of care and attention that should have been provided for her child.

When mom came home, I knew she knew the real story. I could tell I was sooo BUSTED, not as much as you'd think for peeing my pants, but more so for lying. I could tell by the look on her face and the one sentence she said that she knew what really happened that day. The one sentence? "So, Peggy wasn't there today, huh?"

My punishment? Removal of all my fashion forward clothing for a week replaced with jeans and tee-shirts, "and then we'll see," she said. And as you have probably guessed, I loovvved clothes! Still do. Not just clothes, but all the "in" clothes, the "hip" clothes, the "fancy" clothes. What hurt just as much was what followed the punishment. Her reasoning behind the punishment. She said, "If you can't take care of what needs to be taken care of, you have a bigger problem than your outfits."

Since my parents weren't big spankers, they always seemed to have alternative creative ways to get their points across for myself and my siblings. I truly believe me being in a wheelchair literally saved mine and my siblings' butts many, many, many times. I say this because over the years I've heard my mom say, "By the time I got Jen out of the chair with all the belts and straps, either I wasn't mad anymore or I forgot what I was mad about in the first place...or it was just too much work." So, they never really got into the spanking habit. I think my sister and brother should have been a little more grateful and shown a little more appreciation for what I was able to do for them. Life in a wheelchair is not all bad. There are, surprisingly, a few benefits.

    Speaking of being grateful, there are two times that stick out most in my mind when I thought gratitude should have been at its highest level. The first time was when my baby brother came home from the hospital. Now, I know I haven't spoken about my beloved pacifier yet, but it was as essential to my nightly routine as Weezy. If I didn't have my pacifier and Weezy, bedtime was not going to be a pleasant experience for my mom, so you have to understand the significant sacrifice I made for him.

    When we returned home from picking him up from the hospital, a trip that had become the norm for us because all three of us, my sister and my brother were preemie babies and spent a couple to a few weeks residing in the neo-natal nursery while Mom went home to ready our world. Like I said, I was ten weeks early. My sister was "only" four weeks early and my brother was seven weeks early, who, btw is six foot three inches tall, three hundred pounds, and plays rugby like a beast.

    Anyway, when I figured out that he did not have his own pacifier, I believed it imperative that he did, and I gave him mine. Now, I was almost four years old and my pacifier had seen way better days. In fact, my parents had already been trying to sever my relationship with said pacifier for some months with no success. Little did I know that he, my brother, wasn't at all interested in pacifiers. But, as perceptive and clever, or should I say shrewd, as parents can be, they facilitated my selfless move and pretended he did to obtain a long sought-after end result---Me with no pacifier. And I have to admit, those first few nights were pretty rough and long.

On the flip side, my sister, who was probably three at the time, made the mistake of thinking that her big sister would never lead her into dangerous territory, and that all of her ideas were fun and good. That particular event took place while my mother was on the phone, back when phones were attached to the wall and roaming around the house with phone in hand was not an option. When my mom became concerned about the "sound of quiet" she became afraid...very, very, afraid, as I've heard over the years, and hung up the phone. When she reached mine and my sister's bedroom, she saw us in a sea of baby powder. Every. Single. Thing. Was. Covered. In. Baby. Powder.

I had convinced my sister to get the baby powder so we could powder and diaper every baby doll we owned. Now, this might not sound like a "grateful" moment, but it is coming. My mom's first reaction was to give both of us wet washcloths, instructing us to clean up the mess. Have you got this picture in your mind right now? Think about it...powder and water make....... glue, or wet cement. Bad mom choice. The grateful moment came when my mom returned to an even bigger mess than when she had left us alone before. Remember the "too much work to get me out of the wheelchair" comment? Add to that the "you can't spank one without spanking the other" rule of fairness, mom had more work cut out for her than spending energy getting me out of my chair to spank me, therefore, removing the spanking threat for my sister as well.

Finally, here I am able to return back to elaborate on the spaz discussion. (I am wondering right now if you feel a tinge of offence, uneasiness or shock at my continual use of the word-spaz. If so, I apologize, but I do so kind of half intentionally to give you a sense of my own reaction at the time.) At that age I had no idea of the meaning of any of those words my mom had used, except the word that had spaz in it. Kids at school used that word all the time. They used it to make fun of someone else, to separate them from the group, to make them feel stupid, dumb or like "the other", if you will. I couldn't believe my own mother was saying that to me, calling me stupid or dumb or another interchangeable word, retarded.

Somewhere in the first dozen pages or so I have already explained what Cerebral Palsy is in quasi formal, adult fashion with medical terminology. But that definition was not going to fly with a six-year-old. Instead, this was my mom's explanation to me.

"You are in a wheelchair because you were born too early. When babies are born too early their brains sometimes don't have enough time to grow or form all the way. When babies' brains don't get a chance to grow all the way, those don't work well or work at all. In your case, the part of your brain that doesn't work at all is the part that tells your legs how to walk."

Okay, I thought and mulled it over for a few seconds. I understood that idea. "But, Mom, that doesn't explain why you called me a spaz." I returned.

For some reason she laughed. "You're right, kiddo. There is more to it. Remember I said that the brain needs time to grow? Well, the brain also needs something called oxygen, sort of the same as the air we breathe. And if the brain doesn't get enough oxygen some parts of the brain get damaged, not broken, but sort of hurt. There is a certain part of the brain that tells other parts of your body to move, like your arms to go up or down, or turning your head from one side to the other, or opening or closing your hands. These are called "voluntary movements" and most people can do them easily without even thinking about it. People who don't have CP are able to move every part of their body smoothly, like this..."

Then I watched her move her arms in a waving motion, and her head from side to side, and open and close her hands like they were dancing. Then she said, "You try."

And I did, key word, tried. I had to focus on each and every movement. Unlike my mother, I literally had to look at my hands and mentally tell them to open and close. Dancing was never gonna happen! I had to specifically think left and right when I tried to turn my head. But it didn't sway like hers had. Mine jerked from side to side. Then, lifting my arms was a less than positive eye-opening experience. I could throw my hands almost behind my ears (which is not something a person with CP would set as a goal, it's a bad thing) but my elbows and shoulders didn't flex or activate...at all. Needless to say, my brain, damaged or not, hit upon a realization, a fact of MY life and how it differed from...well, probably from almost everyone else.

"You see how much you have to work to move your arms and stuff? And how choppy you are when you do move?" My mother asked. I stared her down but answered in the affirmative. "That, sweet thing, how hard it is for you to control the way you move, the jerky and choppy way you move, is called spasticity or having spastic movements. And because both of your arms and both of your legs, that is four things, are hard for you to control is why they call what you have Spastic Quadriplegic Cerebral Palsy. Spastic means hard to move or jerky. Quad means four. And (ri)plegic means unable to move. Cerebral means the brain, and palsy is a word that means sort of the same as plegic, that there is a problem with the muscles in your body that makes it hard to move."

"So you weren't calling me a spaz?"

"Nope, not at all. It is just the name of your physical condition, the way your body works."

"Okay," I said. As long as she wasn't calling me a spaz I'd accept my mother's explanation, even if I didn't really totally understand it all at the time, and thinking that was the end of all conversations about my "condition." But I was wrong.

I remember several weeks later excitedly going to my mom and asking her if I could get my ears pierced. "Excuse me? What?" was her response.

"Yes! All my friends from school, my 'girl' friends I mean, and me too, want to get our ears pierced," I answered. To be honest, right now, I don't really recall why we all came together wanting to get our ears pierced or where we got the idea. All I remember is we all adamantly wanted to put holes in our ears.

"Ahhhh, no," she stuttered. And before I could cry, throw a fit, or ask why, because I was going to do all three of those things, my mom pointed to the kitchen table where it was a habit for us to have all of our important conversations. If I was allowed to have said "oh crap" right then, I would have. I kinda knew this was going to be a "no" conversation. But I knew it was going to be more than a "because I said so" conversation.

I didn't even have a chance to form the word 'why' before my mom put everything on that dang kitchen table! "Remember that talk we had a few weeks ago about muscle control and the things you can and can't do? Well, one of those muscle things has to do with why you wear dribble rags, bibs. Because you don't have the ability to use the muscles to swallow, you drool." Then she said, "Wait, that isn't exactly right. You can swallow when you drink or when you eat because you are concentrating, thinking about it, paying attention to what you are doing, or at least most of the time." (I did and still do have a tendency to choke if I don't pay attention.)

She went on to explain how the drooling would affect getting my ears pierced in a negative way. You see, I slept on my stomach which meant one side of my face was continually laying on a soggy saliva soaked pillow...which I might add had been stuffed with towels to help soak up some of the spit. My mom then explained that should I get me ears pierced and drool all over the pillow, it, the spit, would get into the holes, get infected and I'd probably lose my ears. Ya, moms do that, exaggerate to prove a point.

Anyway, her scare tactic didn't quite work the way she had intended. In fact, it backfired and had the totally opposite desired effect. In my mind, I was sure I could find a way around the "issue." "What if I stopped drooling? Could I get my ears pierced then?" I asked.

This is one of those examples where and when dads can be soooo cooool! Why? Because mine, unbeknownst to me, had been listening to the discussion the whole time, and picked that moment to interject his parental...I don't know...parental authority or something, I guess, or maybe throw out a challenge. All I knew for sure was that what he said next gave me an opportunity to get what I wanted, and maybe prove that sometimes, even a small accomplishment is a big deal and doable.

What did he say? "If you can keep it dry for a week, I'll take you to get your ears pierced myself," was all he said. A week and a half later I had accomplished a major goal, one that no one thought I could, came home with holes in my ears. The funniest part about the whole thing was that Mom had no say so. It had become a me and Dad deal.

I hadn't even thought about any of the added bonuses of not drooling. Not that a week and a half as a time line is considered immediate gratification, but getting my ears pierced was my only goal, the only goal I was focused on because adding earrings, pierced earrings, to my daily attire would not only support my desire to "be part of the whole", it would surely elevate my level of style. I say part of the whole as in "I am like everyone else", although interestingly, not all of my friends were allowed to get their ears pierced. Actually, a very small number ever showed up at school with pierced ears. Therefore, I never became part of the whole. Instead, I sort of became a member of an elite subgroup who were envied due to social hierarchy of standards...the haves and the have-nots. I, on the other hand, just thought it was me being lucky and having a pretty cool dad. I didn't mind being part of whatever 'this group' was called as opposed to "the other" group I mentioned before, the group separated from the whole for being "less" or perceived different in a bad way.

So, being envied was a bonus and sort of an instant gratification thing as well because it happened pretty fast, faster than a week and a half. The other bonuses that arose from not drooling also played into my...perception of myself, my appearance, and brought me a new found sense of pride, not only of my new accessories but also of my new acceptable behavior, not slobbering all down the front of my clothes. Dare I say, I was proud of my perseverance, my awareness of and being able to change, all by myself, an undesirable behavior. I had such a feeling of accomplishment.

That feeling of accomplishment was surprisingly compounded when my mother ripped off my outfit driven, color coordinated, dribble rag, the bib, I was wearing and announced, "Guess you don't need these anymore?" Then she threw it in the trash along with every other one I owned, which she had secretly collected up in preparation for the epic surprise I had not connected to or expected when I quit drooling.

Can you imagine my excitement at a seemingly small gesture to most, but grandiose to me?! Side note: To punctuate the level of excitement I felt at this action I would like to share that as I sit here writing in Starbucks, yes Starbucks, I **screeched** with joy, way too loudly, at the memory and cause the entire place to go dead silent, slightly embarrassing myself. Eh, not really caring. This also brings up a non-diagnosed, quirk, I guess I'd call it. I have always done that, screech uncontrollably when I get excited. I say undiagnosed because when I do the "screech thing" my parents have always made some kind of comment, in just mind you, about my Tourette(s), something that I had never been diagnosed with. I think it might really be a vocal aspect of the spastic condition more so than Tourette(s). Physically, as explained earlier, is the uncontrollable tightening of muscles and jerky movements. Verbally, I'd guess, it is the uncontrollable emotional muscle, I'm going to call it, which causes the spontaneous outbursts. However, my parents' reference to the Syndrome did and does cause me to pause and collect myself.

After losing a major element of my life-long fashion faux pas, a thought popped into my adolescent head. I started to wonder and question what more could happen, what else could change, what more could I do differently. I only had to wait a few weeks to find out.

I don't recall discussing the strap apparatus that was attached to the orange chair that used to, one, hold me in the chair, and two, helped hold my bibs in place. They were H straps that went across my chest and over each shoulder to strap and hold me upright. A similar setup was added to my electric wheelchair to provide the same support. Without the need for a bib holder, the only thing preventing the world from seeing and appreciating my fashion sense in its entirety was the ugly ole H strap.

One day, out of the blue while washing dishes, (other than the kitchen table that is where we had a lot of our best conversations) my mom hit me with what I thought was a super odd question. She asked if I thought I could sit up.

Like, what?! "I'm in a wheelchair, mom, did you forget? And I've never been able to sit up by myself," was my retort.

She laughed and rebounded with, "no, I didn't forget. Not really what I was getting at. I just had a crazy thought, though." Then she continued. She pointed out that I had recently worked really hard at achieving a goal, one that no one actually thought I could even come close to attaining. "It wasn't just a fluke. You still swallow and don't drool all over yourself," she commented. "And because of that you were able to get your ears pierced, kind of like a reward, I guess."

I was a little proud but also a little confused. I didn't quite understand where my mom was going with all of this. "So, what does that have to do with sitting up?" I asked.

"Okay, well," she started, "since you did something no one thought you could do and because of that you haven't had any issues with your ears, I was wondering if you were ready for another challenge."

"Ah, what is a challenge?" I had to ask. "I don't know what that word means."

"Sorry," mom answered. Then she explained to me that a challenge was kind of like a test or a contest or trying something new to see if you can do "It" (whatever it should happen to be).

"I think I do challenges all the time, Mom," I quipped, "I just didn't know what they were called." And that was an understatement. In reality, my whole life had been one big challenge. Just being alive had been a challenge. Talking intelligibly had been a challenge. Being allowed to go to a regular school had been a challenge. Being accepted as a person had been a challenge. Learning to drive an electric wheelchair had been a challenge. Learning to swallow so I could get my ears pierced had been a challenge. Basically, everything I had ever done or would do would be a challenge.

"Well, are you ready for a new one?" she asked. I answered in the affirmative and she laid out the new challenge for me.

What she proposed was me being able to get rid of the H strap tie-down harness, or at least part of it. My mother's question about being able to sit up now made perfect sense. She explained that if I was capable of holding an upright sitting position in my chair I could theoretically have one less obnoxious and confining, adaptive apparatus. By now you have to know that the less there was covering up my clothes, the happier I was. I had dreamt of that happening for a long time, like forever! Not necessarily losing the straps per say, but being able to let my inner diva shine through my outer style.

And so the challenge began. The shoulder straps came down and I worked diligently to keep my upper body in the acceptable up-right position. I had no problem with holding the front to back stability I needed. I did, however, have to work very hard to, believe it or not, build up enough core strength to conquer the side to side stability needed to hold myself up. It seemed like forever, but a couple of weeks later I had a new frilly blouse as a reward for killing the challenge!

Speaking of inner diva and labels people are given or give themselves, my grandpa, although not a diva, did have a label. My grandpa was and had always been, among other things, a salesman. We always said he could "sell a bald-headed man a brush and make him think he had hair." I mention this as a segue into my career as a Brownie. I never made it into Girl Scouts and I'll explain that later.

Brownies was, and I am assuming still is, (I was going to say "loosely based", but I think actually "based" is a better description, so) based on a goal, challenge, achievement and reward system. Now, you have to understand, that was right up my alley! That was a way of life for me. All the things I've described previously; sucking through a straw, blowing bubbles, using the toilet, swallowing and sitting upright in my wheelchair, for example, were all goal based challenges that I achieved and was rewarded for in some way. It would never cross most peoples' minds that sucking chocolate milk through a straw would be a challenge or something to be rewarded for. So, earning achievement badges or patches was just a warm up for me...for a couple of reasons. The first being cookie sales. Now, look at the cover of the book you have in your hands. Cute factor, right? You have to admit, I had it. Who could say no to that face? I sold literally hundreds of boxes of cookies.

In fact, (okay, so this is where my salesman grandpa comes into the story) when at an extended family gathering where I was also delivering a case of cookies to my grandpa I was accused of following in his footsteps and pulling a fast one over on him. Also in attendance at this gathering was a second cousin who had not had the chance to order cookies. He wanted some. I came up with the most brilliant idea. I went to my "salesman" grandpa and asked him if I could resell a few of his boxes of cookies to Cameron, my second cousin. He, of course, said yes and I proceeded to present them to Cameron, charged him the appropriate amount for the cookies, and promptly asked him to please put the money in my bag.

"Hey, hey," where's my money?" My grandpa laughed.

"In my bag," I seriously responded which was followed by a room full of laughter.

"That's your granddaughter, Parr," my grandmother flatly stated. "She didn't fall far from the 'I got the best of you' tree!"

The second reason I considered and excelled at, I might add, earning badges in Brownies a warm up was because it was the beginning, the first step towards my newly realized ability to think about how to get something done that I couldn't physically do myself and manipulate situations to my advantage. Ya, I know, most kids learn early on how to manipulate people, especially parents. I'm talking about something a little different. Something more than the everyday ploy just to get a cookie without finishing my dinner.

Some people would use the word manipulate. I think convince, compromise, and negotiation would be a better string of words to use. Stop laughing! Yes, it still sounds like manipulate, but let me give you an example of what I mean.

The first thing that comes to mind is way off the semi sort of established timeline of this narrative. But it is an excellent representation of what I'm trying to say. When I was in high school there was an opportunity for me to become the FFA barn foreman, a paid position. The job included a variety of physical tasks such as sweeping, raking leaves, scrubbing out water troughs, animal inoculations, breeding of school owned animals, delivery of newborn animals (along with my own), and so much more. Obviously, there was no way I was capable of attempting, much less completing, any of those physical tasks that came with the job. The way I solved this problem was to approach my mother with a proposal, one that would take compromising by both parties. I convinced her to let me take the job with the contingency that she would be my hands, my legs, my back, my physical strength for which we negotiated payment for her services out of my paycheck.

You might think that was the whole of the job and I was getting paid for doing nothing. Not true. My part of the deal, the job, was the cognitive, the cerebral part of the job. For me to use the word cerebral, as in Palsy here, as in doesn't work, may sound weird to you, I know. And not that I am a terribly religious person, but have you ever heard the saying, "What God takes away He replaces with something else?" What I'm trying to say is that my cognitive, my 'mental function' and capacity was and has always been well above average. (Some might even call me a tad obsessive compulsive because of the way I run scenarios with possible results through my head, and the way I can move fluidly from plan A to plan B.) Anyway, my portion of the job was thought-based while my mother's portion was based on the physical. I was the decision maker, the schedule preparer, the record keeper, the routine setter, the organizer and planner. Ultimately, I was the one held responsible for what did and didn't go down at the barn because the person really in charge, my Ag. Teacher, didn't care how things got done to her satisfaction, just that they got done to her satisfaction.

Brownies, cookies, grandpa, and barn stories aside, I suppose I should revisit the concept of a life full of everyday challenges and growing up differently-abled, and how my family and I approached them and what strategies were used to meet and hopefully "smash" said challenges. I say hopefully because not every challenge was smashable. The idea of "something is better than nothing" would appropriately fit here because conventional thinking states that "this is how it should be done", and guess what, it ain't! I can't help but question and "challenge" the idea of conventional thinking with a couple of words…normal and adaptation. I have to say it---one person's normal is another person's adaption.

What I do may be different, but not wrong. I am looking for the same end result as any other person. How I get there is basically, in my opinion, irrelevant. Some people are left handed and others are right handed. The end result is the same, the ability to write or something close to it. Different, yes, but which is right and which is wrong? They both get a sentence written, although the handwriting and sentences are undoubtedly completely un-alike. Another example is the art form of pottery. Here there are two avenues which potters prefer, the wheel thrown vs hand built. Neither is right or wrong, just different, again with probable end results varying in style or type, but still a completed masterpiece. One of my personal examples would be that of writing with a computer and arm brace, which was actually a skate boarding wrist guard with a pencil attached. When my classmates would take pencil to paper to practice spelling words by writing them ten times each, I would peck them out, letter by letter, on my computer...ten times each.

Here I'd also like to share some of the teaching techniques that my parents stumbled upon during my early scholastic years. Think about this for a minute...most children learn (even if you tell them not to) to count, add, and so forth by using their fingers. It is an absolute visual thing. Because I was unable to use my digits in that fashion due to my disability, I didn't have a concrete concept, a visual connection, of and to numbers. Somehow my mom figured out how to teach me visually with "things" other that my fingers. She substituted crayons for fingers, laying them on the table for me to see and count. Later on we used crackers to learn fractions. When learning and studying geography I learned about pairing...the boot and below were Italy and Greece. And when the time came, I learned and still find myself using today, something we called "the 9 trick." That trick begins "9 plus anything is one less in the teens" and I'll let you figure out the rest. They funny thing about all of the adaptive teaching techniques my parents came up with specifically for me, turns out, were as usable and helpful with my able-bodied siblings. Turns out, adaptive learning isn't just for the disabled. As each circumstance arose, each challenge, it was looked at and evaluated using a trial and error methodology, a methodology that my parents happily shared with other parents.

    To expand on the topic of making and implementing adaptions, school and academics was not an isolated time or place where my parents did so as you have probably picked up on by now. Being included in extra-curricular activities was always important for my entire family. Instead of just listing them, take a second here and flip back to the pictures, a visual record of what I'm talking about and what you may be questioning or doubting actually happened. Yep, that is all me...me in an effort to be and do normal things. There is that word -normal-. It is such a relative term. My normal is way different than most of my friends' normal, and not generally envied, my normal, that is.

But envied I was, as weird as that sounds. It's a double-edged sword phenomenon, of sorts. Sometime around third or fourth grade, gosh, I don't even remember, but some organization invited me to attend a big car racing event as a guest. The invitation was extended to me as if I were that organization's project or "do good cause." Don't get me wrong. I had a blast. Of course my dad had to go with me and he had a blast, as well. The counter to that experience was hearing from both my siblings and my peers that it was unfair that I got to go because of my "special needs", my being in a wheelchair. They thought I was lucky for being disabled and in a wheelchair because it afforded me some special treatment. Ahhh, special treatment? I'm going to be a little blunt and well, maybe gross, here. Special treatment, like I've had to have someone wipe my butt since the day I was born. Now that is special!

Later that year, the flip side of the previous situation arose in which my wheelchair was the center of all things. In this instance, the chair was unseen, literally and figuratively. Psycho-babble, right? Not really. That Halloween my dad came up with the coolest costume for me, ever. We happened to have a refrigerator box from a newly delivered refrigerator that my dad creatively channeled into the blue racecar number eighteen, a replica of the car I rooted for at the races a couple of months before. The box fit over my entire chair as I sat inside as the driver...chair unseen, disability unseen. My point here? In the attempt to be and look "normal", I was again envied, not because I got special treatment for being in a wheelchair, but because when trying to make the best of a bad situation, being in a wheelchair, I had the coolest costume out of everyone. While attending my high school reunion some years ago the field trip to the race track had long been forgotten. What was remembered and the topic of conversation for some time was the year that I 'was' a racecar.

    And therein lies a whole other interesting realization for me. Friends: who they are, why they are, what they see, and how they act or react towards me or others for or because of me. I've already mentioned, Janice, as a best buddy. Janice, who without pause, included me from day one. She always used and incorporated what I had to offer as a contributing member of "our" neighborhood group. I was never any different.
    Another friend for life bestie, Matt Perkins, I met while being mainstreamed from my special education kindergarten class into his first grade classroom. Neither of us remember why or how our friendship began. I know this because I Facebook messaged him to obtain permission to use his name in the book and asked if he did because I didn't. We both recall the fact that I sat in his lap on the floor during some sort of circle time gathering, a daily routine activity. Although, we both guessed that his mother probably had something to do with it since she was room-mother at the time, and that was just the kind of person she was. As Janice was my best and true home buddy, Matt was my first best and true school buddy, later to become my trouble making partner.
    Anyway, what I'm getting at is the difference I found between "true friends",

sometimes those that are also family, and "acquaintances" or those that found me too different and undeserving of taking up space on this earth...also sometimes family (harsh statement, I know, but so terribly honest) True friends, not necessarily best friends mind you, those who took the time to know me eventually never saw my wheelchair. They just saw me, and from day one that has never changed. I may have been described or known as "Jenni in the wheelchair," but that was just that, a description, like saying "Jenny from the block" or the blonde girl with pink glasses...yes I had pink glasses, and they were pinkalicious before there was such a thing.

Another example of kids or people giving me a chance, I guess I'd say in some weird or awkward way, and proving myself as worthy of friendship, was when I met a boy named Andrew Fears. I met Andrew in fourth grade. By that time, it was pretty evident that all the physical and occupational therapy I'd had and that was still part of my weekly routine was not going to miraculously or magically assist me in standing up one day and walking. I was what I am. My physical condition had not changed much, nor had abilities such as the speed of typing improved.

Even though not much had improved or changed as far as my physical capabilities, it was still believed imperative for me to have "out of chair time" during the day to get a chance to stretch out and hopefully slow down the inevitable tightening and contracting of muscles. It was during those out of chair times, when I was laid on a mat, on the floor, with a classmate volunteer during free read time, that I became friends with Andrew. He was the first to volunteer, among others, but soon took over the task from the class as his own. My other classmates lost interest in the job, or me, for whatever reason.

In that one-on-one time, when Andrew sat on the mat next to me, when we should have been reading, we learned about each other. He was never afraid of me and always open to me being me. He had the patience to give me the time I needed to talk, and he listened. When the time came for students to pair up for the school's science fair it was a no-brainer for Andrew. He just assumed he and I would be working on a project together. We were almost inseparable, like a grade school "thing," I look back now and think I thought of him as my first boyfriend or the sweetest, kindest boy ever.

I'm not really sure what attributes each of these three people have, but there was something brought out in them, maybe because of me, I think, that drew them to me. Maybe it was a kindness in them, a desire to help, a simple curiosity, a supportive and inclusive outlook or blindness, in my case, to my differences or inabilities...and me to them because of their general attitude, actions, and respect to and for me.

Here are a couple of short stories about blindness. I have two cousins that I have been close to all of our lives. I've heard stories about us...them...and how they responded to me and or wheelchairs.

Story one:

> When our families got together our parents had to really keep a close eye on us. I'm told that many-a-time my cousins were caught in the act of attempting to remove me from my wheelchair. They wanted me to be on the floor playing with them. The wheelchair was just in the way. They never fully succeeded in their mission, but totally succeeded in the conscious thought and act of inclusion.

Story number two:

> The same two cousins were out grocery shopping with their mom when they spotted a wheelchair that looked like mine in the checkout line. They, of course, thought it was me and ran up to say hi and talk. When they realized the person in the wheelchair was not me they took a breath's pause, and to the stunned woman in the wheelchair's sheer delight, kept talking to

her. My aunt, their mother, rather embarrassed, ran to apologize for her children's bold and possibly intrusive behavior. To my aunt's surprise, the woman who happened to have a dog in her lap, similar to the one I always had in my lap, had a huge smile on her face and giant tears in her eyes.

The woman proceeded to grasp my aunt's hand and said, "Oh please, let them stay." As it turns out the woman was extremely shocked and pleased at the same time, not by, but because of my cousin's unabashed actions. The woman explained that no one had ever approached her without solicitation so unafraid and willing to accept her as she was. Of course, my aunt then shared the fact that she had a niece who had CP and was also in a wheelchair. She explained that her boys had been around me all their lives and had no inclination to suspect or understand that I was all that different than the rest of the world. To them this lady was just a lady with a dog in her lap.

After thinking about this for a few minutes, the "just a lady with a dog in her lap sitting in a wheelchair" scenario for my cousins would easily be comparable to a non-wheelchair scenario. The best way for me to explain it would be this: You know someone with dark curly hair, about 5'6" tall who usually wears black yoga pants and a tye-dyed tee-shirt. One day you are out shopping and see this person, a really cool person, no doubt, standing in a checkout line. You haven't seen her for a while, so you run up to give her a big hug. Low and behold, it isn't your yoga pants, tye-dye wearing friend. After turning fourteen shades of red and apologizing profusely, you strike up a conversation with this woman and discover that she is a really super cool person and that you are glad you met her...no matter the circumstances.

All this reflecting and supposing reminds me of an experiment my mom has always wanted to do. Some years ago, okay, many years ago, she noticed that there seemed to be an age break at which time children no longer accepted me as 'not usual' and/or approachable. My cousins, having grown up with me and having the assumption, and believing that I was as right and normal as rain, were and are not, in fact, the norm. As I stated a few paragraphs earlier, the norm would be closer to the idea of being undeserving of taking up space on this earth. That may be a little harsh, but in truth, it's no harsher than being looked at side-eyed and backed away from by people because those (I have to add UNEDUCATED here) people believe they could catch what you have. Yep, more people than you would imagine believe that it is possible to catch my disability because I was born too early.

Okay, so back to the experiment. I'm going to make a blanket statement out of the blue here. *Prejudice is a learned behavior.* What does that have to do with anything? In my thirty-some-odd years of experiences in life as a disabled person, if I have seen nothing else, I have seen an absolute difference in the way young children react, respond, and interact with me, a person in a wheelchair, in contrast to that of older children and adults. I'd kind of like to say "or lack thereof" when referring to the behavior of, probably, most adults.

Now, I have no actual scientific proof or thesis or documented evidence of what I just said, but really, isn't life a laboratory?! And that is where my mom's experiment comes in. She had always wanted to go to a busy mall, position me in a somewhat high traffic area, hide and watch. Her question? When, at what age do children take direction, and learn from their parents not to interact with a person, in my case, in a wheelchair? She has always wanted to know when that lesson is learned. Again, there is no scientific proof to my knowledge, but my experiences have shown me that young children have no fear, no preconceived notions, and are not intimidated by my condition or appearance. In fact, my being in a wheelchair has often resulted in just the opposite. Ya know that saying, "I'm a chick magnet"? Well me and my chair, we "are a kid magnet."

What the heck does that mean? First of all, it means just what it sounds like. Little kids are attracted to, I want to say me, but in reality, they, especially little boys, are attracted to my wheelchair, as in get their hands on it. I'm going to make a wee bit of a gender generalization here which is so wrong and the opposite of all my inclusion based beliefs. But, there is just something that happens, a curiosity, when little boys, no, I think in reality all boys see anything with wheels, or knobs, or switches. I'm talking from age, well, crawling age to...hummm....I don't seem to have a top age. But you get where I'm going, right? A natural attraction. On more occasions than I can count, when at some gathering, I've had little fingers pulling cables, pushing buttons, twisting wheels and knobs with an intense fascination. And there is no stopping any of them. In the beginning we tried. Now we just watch, laugh, and make sure nothing gets unplugged or broken, and eventually they lose interest and wonder off. Just like when I entered kindergarten, initially I'm an oddity and a big deal but only for a little while.

    Since I singled out the male gender, let me give equal time to the female. Although not as "hands-y", girls are no less aware of, interested in and inquisitive about my wheelchair and why I'm in it. Let me tell you one of my favorite little girl interactive stories.

    One day while shopping with my sister and her kids (this is years down the road from where we actually are in the timeline of the book, but it is a perfect example) one of them had to use the restroom. My mom and I offered to take her while my sister and the other kids continued shopping. As we approached the restrooms we passed a grandmother-aged woman with a girl of about four or five years old sitting in the front of the shopping cart. The little girl, as loud as her little voice would carry asked, "Grandma, what's wrong with that girl?"

    The grandmother was visibly embarrassed and attempted to hush the girl by putting her hand over the child's mouth and saying "SSHHHHHH," all while not making any eye contact, whatsoever. Being pretty proactive when it comes to answering children's questions in general, my mom gave the grandmother one of my book writing business cards. I'm a published author of children's books, most of which have some kind of disability element to them. She briefly explained to the grandmother that should she need help in explaining the wheelchair to her granddaughter, this website and these books might help.

Meanwhile, my niece, after witnessing what had just transpired, asked my mom, her grandmother, "What's wrong with THAT girl? There's nothin' wrong with Aunt Jenni!" As we got closer to the restrooms she noticed the wheelchair/handicapped emblem on the, I guess you'd call it the family restroom door, and was exquisitely amazed and excited by the sight of it, and declared, "Look, there's a wheelchair on the emblem on the door. That means it's for Aunt Jenni to use, too. We can all use it together." I say exquisitely because she also around the age of five, already had an inclusive mindset when it came to me, her wheelchair-bound aunt.

After all the talk about boys and girls, and children and adults, I think the outcome of my mom's experiment would boil down to outside influences and how receptive children are to adults' direction opposed to their natural inquisitiveness. Over the years I have come to understand that a negative attitude is not the natural state of being. Now I'm throwing my philosophical thoughts in here. If it's too much skip ahead.

I mentioned prejudice being a learned behavior, a learned behavior due, I believe, to fear, ignorance, and a skewed point of view, behavior children learn from adults who, more often than not, have no honest, informative knowledge. I mean how many times does a kid need to hear the words "don't look at her, don't talk to her, don't go around her" about a person in a wheelchair without instilling a negative view of "her."

Because most adults, parents, teachers, or what have you, have no interaction with disabled people, they have nothing to draw from when asked even the simplest questions. They avoid, ignore, and shut down the natural inquisitiveness of any child. And I have to say, the inquisitive nature of a child absolutely goes hand in hand with the lack of a filter. I for one, love a child without a filter.

Over the years, those are the children that became my true friends, my besties. The ones that didn't have filters. Those like Marco who got up in my face and asked me whatever it was that was on his mind at the moment. He was the one who asked the questions others were afraid to ask but wanted to know. I suppose most folks, able-bodied or disabled, would be offended by up close, in your face, possibly personal, none of your business inquires. But in all honesty, I've always much preferred a kid that runs up to me and asks why I'm in a wheelchair than the alternative---being ignored.

Although Marco was not one of my best friends, his candor and open mouth quality absolutely led to the open flow of communication for at least my peers. My closest and best friends were open to, and invested time in, me. Why? I don't even know. I'd like to think it had something to do them having a kind heart coupled with compassion. But I'm just guessing. I'm not talking about feeling sorry for me. I'm talking about believing I could do "it", whatever "it" was or may have been. Maybe they each found a uniqueness in me other than my disability. Thinking back now I remember how each sort of saw a desire, a need, a want, an ability, an aptitude...for something. Actually, I don't really know how to explain why or what the heck drew them to me, but they were drawn to me and me to them. But what I can tell you is my life would not have been the same had I not had them in my life.

For example, my friend Matt, who was not as boisterous as Marco, came back into my life some years after our kindergarten friendship. We reconnected again when I decided I wanted to show sheep...and that was my grandmother's fault. Okay, you're going to need a little background here 'cause showing sheep has just been pulled in from way out of left field.

So, somewhere around the age of nine, fourth-grade-ish, my grandmother had decided that my mom needed to have all, and I mean all of her 4-H trophies. Grandma and Grandpa had either decided they didn't need or want to be mom's storage locker any more, thought Mom should have her childhood keepsakes, or maybe they were moving and just didn't want to move my mom's crap with them. All I know is Grandma showed up at our house one day with several boxes of trophies. There were all kinds of trophies, trophies won from Santa Clara County Fair exhibits. There were trophies for sewing, canning, cooking, baking, chickens, yep, you read that right, chickens, sheep, beef, and horses. These were all thing my mom had won a Best of Fair Award for, as well as the biggest trophy of all, something called The Round Robin trophy, a trophy that the entire animal showing 4-H community coveted. That was it. I was done. I wanted to do what my mother had done. I wanted my own Round Robin trophy.

To my mother's chagrin and snake eye to my grandmother, I remember my mom sighing heavily and saying what she always said when I wanted to do something, pretty much anything that was probably outside of my realm of capabilities, "Okay, well give it a shot, kiddo." And that was the end of my Brownie career. Sorry Grandpa, no more $2.50 boxes of cookies. Things were going to get a lot more expensive.

Now, one would have thought the actual showing of animals would have been the hard part. So wrong! The hard part was finding a 4-H club that felt comfortable and accepting of a kid in a wheelchair. We went from club to club, being turned down by each because of all of the things I have previously discussed; fear, ignorance …la, la, la, same ole, same ole. Then we finally found Westside 4-H where I hooked up with Matt Perkins and his mom again, the place I finally found where I was not only accepted, but where I was supposed to be. The rest is history.

Reconnecting with Matt and his mom, joined by his father, he whom after a short period of time we began to call "God" because he knew all there was to know about sheep, at least to a nine-year-old, was not only just destined to happen, but was probably fate as well. Matt, by now was a sheep "G" in training and my biggest champion. I wanted to show sheep and nothing was going to stop him from making sure that I, first and foremost, would be in the show ring, come hell or high water.

When other 4-H "people", mostly adults and parents, approached and questioned Matt and his family about the reasoning behind me being allowed to participate, my ability to participate, in the 4-H program, because, for heaven's sake what could I possibly be able to do, Matt's answer was plain and simple. "Why can't she do it?" To which those people, highly competitive and cutthroat on their own children's behalf I might add, fumbled and mumbled to come up with any real explanation for their claim.

In reality, the problem didn't have so much to do with what I could or couldn't do, but more with the perceived advantage I would be afforded by being in a wheelchair along with being nestled snuggly under the wing of one of the most knowledgeable, competitive, winning, and probably feared families in the sheep show ring on earth. There was a saying, and probably still is, among the livestock community. Along with being a jab, it was also a backhanded compliment. Basically, it meant if you were good at what you did in the animal world…winning, you simultaneously became a bad person. The saying, "If you are good, you are bad", was a phrase Matt, at nine or ten years old, was already hearing. And it wasn't long before I heard those same words in reference to myself.

The thing is, the Perkins family didn't, like most people assume, (and you all know what that word breaks down too, not so much me, just the 'you part') just give "it" to me. I had to work and learn all, and I mean all about sheep. Before I even got a sheep, (or a lamb to be more precise because that is what a young sheep is called) to show, I had to learn about feed ratios, pound to pound feed weight gain, percentage of fat coverage preferred, the need for and which supplements were needed, and that is just the feeding of the animals. Then I had to learn and understand which were the most desirable cuts of meat and why. And that was just the book learning.

After that came the somewhat more challenging task of teaching me how to decipher the animals' conformation. Why more challenging? Because in order to do so, one must be able to physically feel with their hands and measure the animal for things like length, depth and thickness of the loin, the circumference of the leg, the fat coverage, and so forth, of all the prime cuts. Since that was and has always been a major obstacle all my life, Matt, coached by his dad, remember "God", taught me how to watch him handle the animal and visually determine what he was feeling and measuring by what I was seeing him do with his hands. Although, when it came to feeling for fat coverage and muscling, it was not beyond Matt to somehow get me out of my wheelchair and hold me up next to the lamb, guide my arm over the top of the animal's back and make me feel for myself. The theory, either developed by Matt or his dad, was that if I could, I needed to. In other words, it was a collaborative effort.

The magical, absolutely hysterical part about the way I learned to translate my visual ability into what others used their physical ability for totally mystified them. The only way I can explain this is that my mental capacity and/or capability has always been totally intact. Even at that early age, probably due to how we used crayons and crackers to learn math, I was able to sort of visualize and compartmentalize each animal, kind of dissect them, evaluate, and then put them back together, placing them in my "visual memory" from best to worst. Actually, the new television series, *The Good Doctor,* staring Freddie Highmore as an autistic surgical resident pretty much demonstrates how my brain process works, but not so much with numbers. That character has something called Autistic Savant syndrome due to brain damage of some sort. Someone with this condition demonstrates certain abilities way above average, especially when having or being taught detailed knowledge in a specific field. In my particular instance it was sheep conformation education. Now, I do not have autism, nor do I claim to be in any way, shape, or form, a savant, but I do seem to have savant level skills or tendencies when it comes to memory.

Not many, or anyone for that matter, understood how I could judge by watching other peoples' hands handle and measure an animal. No one believed how, or that it was possible for me to visually remember what I saw, then compare one animal to another, as in a judging competition, and score somewhere near the top... every single time. I noticed that I sometimes even amazed Matt and his dad, watching them smirk and shake their heads from the back of the crowd. I think I made them proud.

This may all sound like unimportant dribble and me just going down memory lane, but what I'm trying to say and show is that there are always different ways of experiencing the same things as others...just adaptively. That it, whatever "it" is, is always doable if you find the right people to support, teach, help and defend your right to do so. Matt and his family were my first such people.

Curt was another one of those people. He was a horse trainer who could not see any reason why I could not ride and show horses. You have to understand that my mom and aunt both showed horses for many years, so it was only natural that I, like the sheep showing, wanted to do the same. My sister was already taking riding lessons from Curt as I sat on the outside of the riding arena. Long story short, my mom enlisted the help of her coworkers to take an old high-back saddle she'd found to manufacture and attach a supportive brace. She, now I know, reluctantly, presented it to Curt and I to test. With the reins tied together in a knot so I could hold them, Curt lead me around the arena for a few minutes until Curt and I felt comfortable. Then to my mother's horror, he removed the lead rope and let me go. A few words were excitedly, and not a good excitedly, exchanged between my mother and Curt. Ultimately, Curt was able to calm my mom down providing her with the knowledge and comfort that I was, in fact, in a safe environment, with the added testament of "look how happy she is and how much fun she is having." Curt later reinforced the idea of this activity with the mention of the therapeutic properties horseback riding possessed for a physically disabled person's muscular and skeletal systems. It was only a few weeks later that I participated in my first horse show in the lead-line class. I sported my new mustard colored chaps, hat, and yellow floral print short. If I was going to do it, I was going to do it all the way. That's just the way we roll...dress the part...all or nothing.

This seems to be a good time to explain my family's philosophy on the idea of participation and inclusion. It was never one sided. I think I've mentioned the phrase "we'll give it a shot." And we gave me a lot of shots, sometimes from multiple angles and directions. When I wanted to do or try an activity of some nature my parents were always game. But once in a while it flipped. Sometimes my family or someone in my family had an activity they wanted to do and wanted and needed to provide me with the ability to be included, if I wanted to or not. It was one of those "command performance" things, if you know what I mean. One of those "You are a member of this family, therefore, you are going to support and participate in a family or sibling activity" thing. I learned early on, as much as I may have wanted to believe, life wasn't all about me all of the time, which looking back on now was a really good thing. One such activity was something as simple as going on a family bike ride.

My dad has always been an avid bicyclist. My sister and brother had bicycles, actually tricycles, way before they were big enough to ride without giant blocks of wood attached to the pedals. I, on the other hand, never had my own bike. I had several varying bicycling contraptions that I rode in or upon to enjoy and share the bicycling experience with my family. Since bicycling was a passion for my dad, he started me out in a bike trailer that my orange chair was strapped into. We would ride around town and along country roads, and he'd point out birds or blossoms on trees or anything else he thought was a point of interest...or to just keep me engaged now that I think about it with an adult mind. That tricky dude!

He used to refer to our bike excursions as "airing me out", meaning getting me out of the house into the fresh air. Spending time outside was another thing my parents were big supporters of all of us kids doing, outdoor activities. But it didn't always work out as well as planned. The story of one instance I have heard repeatedly is the time I threw up while riding home from pre-school in the bicycle trailer, an almost everyday occurrence. The riding home part, not the throwing up part.

You have to understand that there were several issues beside the obvious, gross, throwing up all over myself and the inside of the trailer. First of all, I had never thrown up before and had no clue what was going on. I must have thought I was on the verge of dying. Secondly, this was back in the day before cell phones were in everyone's pocket or purse, so my dad had no way to contact my mom for a car rescue. He could have gone back to school and used the phone there, but he was halfway home. Six of one and half a dozen of another. He decided to keep going. After cleaning me up the best he could and calming me down, we forged forward, while he kept my mind occupied with other things besides puke. Once home, and I have to stress that it was summertime, I got a full-fledged front yard garden hose shower. As wonderful as my mother was and is, she was not having it. What it? Having my dad carrying me from the garage, though the kitchen, through the living room, and down the hall to the bathroom, dripping in vomit. There are just some things that are and are not going to happen...able-bodied or not. I'm thinking I was just glad it was one-hundred degrees outside, and hoped I hadn't ruined my outfit.

By the time I was in grade school bicycling was no longer a feasible mode of transportation for my dad and I. There were now three of us; me, my sister, and my little brother, all going to different schools, part of the time with different start and ending schedules. That's when I learned about the school bus.

I had several bus drivers over several years, but Jim, aka, Roadrunner, was my favorite, and I was his guinea pig. He had been a bus driver for years, but never a "special needs" bus driver. He had never attempted a four-point tie-down before, so he came to my house the day before I started fourth-grade to practice loading, unloading, and hooking up the wheelchair restraints to hold and stabilize a wheelchair to the floor of the bus. I hate, by the way, the term "special needs." Just a personal peeve of mine. Instead of being **identified** as special needs, I'd much rather be **described** as "Jenni in the wheelchair" like anyone else would be described by a physical aspect. I could have easily been described as Jenni with the pink glasses. Yes, I get that I have more intense needs than most people, but who doesn't at some point in time.

    Now, back to Jim. After spending the day together, we became fast friends. Friends to the degree that I earned the nickname, Snoozer, because I fell asleep on the bus <u>one time</u> and he never let me forget it. I christened him with the nickname of Roadrunner because that what he did all day long...run up and down the road all day long picking up and delivering kids either at school, therapy or home. I was the only one he drove during my route for a while. Shortly thereafter, we were joined by Andrea, better known as Slugger (can you guess why) and Matthew in the wheelchair, better known as spitter (also, can you guess why). I get now that giving out those particular nicknames were highly insensitive and rude, but it was Jim's way, I think, of protecting and distracting me from freaking out about being slugged or spit on. More times than not, my slightly off kilter sense of humor has gotten me through a lot of difficult angst, and nerve racking situations. Lucky for me, Jim had the same skewed sense of humor and understood what I needed and how to provide and assist me.

To double the trouble and further bond our relationship, our birthdays were a day apart, and we always tried to out-do each other in gifts. Remember, he was an adult and I was a kid. But, somewhere around the sixth-grade, I was able to outdo and out think an adult. I won. I claimed the title of giving the best gift, ever! And I was pretty proud of the fact that I was even able to pull it off.

I'd conned Jim into meeting myself and a whole gang of other people at my house. We then, as a crowd of giggling women and girls, ushered a frightened Jim down the street to the neighborhood hairdresser as he skittishly, but proudly, held onto his red ponytail, where they happen to also pierce ears. After hearing a story that Jim had had an ear pierced years and years before, and because he owned a motorcycle shop where he was generally covered in grease and grime, he had let it grow closed because of constant infection. Yep, my gift to him that year was to have the piercing redone for him. Under only a tiny bit of protest, he happily relented and led us home sporting a glimmering silver post.

I mention this friendship as an example of my developing sense of knowing and awareness. What I'm getting at is that "the all about me thing" was beginning to be trumped by my desire to do for others. I guess I was beginning to understand how doing for and with others was a different type of inclusion. I sort of want to call it a "reverse inclusion." It was me being part of a group without it being because, about, or for me.

Another example of my newly coined term, reverse inclusion, that I'd like to share, would be the sixth-grade science camp trip in the Santa Cruz mountains. Understand that me going to science camp was a two-fold inclusionary experience. First of all, my mom not only had to drive me there in our personal vehicle, but for obvious reasons, she also had to stay and camp for what she called THE. WHOLE.ENTIRE.WEEK. in the cold and rain, with way too many kids! Again, that is the way both of my parents rolled. Their personal comfort never stood in the way of my chance to be included in any given activity.

The second half of this particular two-fold experience presented itself when we were divided up into what were called survival groups. The scenario: Lost in the forest. There was going to be a torrential downpour. Build a "satisfactory" shelter with what we had on our person or what we could find. (Hey, we were survivors before *Survivor* was a television show!) Getting back to the story, my person was substantially bigger than everyone else's person, me being in a wheelchair with a backpack full of things like a banana yellow rain poncho, electrical tape, twine, straws, and probably a foldable screwdriver. The reverse inclusion? They, all of the groups, wanted and needed me for what I could contribute to the survival exercise. If I remember correctly, and I'm sure I do, my group, "our" group had the best shelter, although we may have been accused of having an unfair advantage. How about that! I was considered an advantage...go figure.

Coming home from science camp with an enthusiastic, positive, all-inclusive attitude about myself and fellow schoolmates came to a screeching halt when I came face to face with Bobby. Bobby my daily tormenter.

I'm not even sure when or how it started, but for some reason, Bobby found great pleasure in seeing me react, being afraid of his, gosh, I almost want to say abusive behavior. I've already discussed my spastic and startle reflex, something Bobby found out about and took advantage of for his own personal entertainment. Initially, I tried to blow if off thinking he'd stop soon. When he didn't and my mom saw the bruises from my wrists to my elbows, we started up the administrative ladder. I have to add that this was after my sister, two years behind me in school, mind you, had already come to my defense in an attempt to rectify the situation, the bullying, harassing and abusive behavior Bobby was inflicting upon me. When our combined forces didn't make a difference is when we started up the ladder and went to my teacher, Mrs. B as we called her. She in turn talked to Bobby and then the principle of the school when there was no change in Bobby's behavior towards me.

Now, I've talked about Matt's dad being dubbed God when it came to the world of sheep, but I have to tell you, I've had more than one god. My first one was and is my own dad. Without giving away my dad's profession, he was intimately knowledgeable when it came to laws, codes and statutes. After hearing the background of what had transpired up until that time, my dad stepped in. I'm talking about going to the top game player here.

So, this is what went down I'm told. Armed with book in hand and several passages marked and highlighted in some obnoxious book of laws and regulations, my parents marched into the principal's office and asked about his knowledge of

Bobby's hazing, harassing, and bullying behaviors and infractions towards their daughter. Foolishly, in my opinion, the principle admitted to knowing about the issue and I have to say, just plain ass dumb, to knowing how long it had been going on.

That was all my dad needed to hear. Even more proactive than my mother had been with the blowing and sucking incident years earlier, my dad opened the book and read one paragraph and one paragraph only. I'm paraphrasing here, but it said something to the effect of---if hazing or harassing is going on at or in a public institution and the administration or people in charge of that institution are aware of these circumstances and do nothing to correct or halt said behavior or action, THAT INSTITUTION MAY BE CLOSED. My dad dropped the book on the principle's desk, I gotta say it, he dropped the mic, and walked out the door with my mom on his arm. I never saw Bobby again.

Even though Bobby was a bully, he was the exception to the rule. Most of my classmates were kind, respectful, and compassionate towards me, and even really considerate about including me in all things going on in the classroom. And although that was the overall desired level of inclusion and participation for me, it was also my whole sixth-grade class, teacher included, who learned that total inclusion was not always in my best interest. One time in particular comes to mind.

Because we were having a pizza party as some kind of goal reaching reward, it was kind of a "blow off the afternoon" kind of day. I had volunteered to bring paper plates, which my mom was going to bring later while other kids brought soda, candy, and other goodies. One of the girls in class offered me a round, hard, throat size, piece of yellow butterscotch candy. You know where this is going, right? Yes, Mr. Heimlich and I became acquainted that day. Not friends, just acquaintances because I didn't really care for him. Besides the obvious, he caused my new party dress to get all bunched up and wrinkled, not to mention, made me get sticky stuff all over myself.

    The call my mother received from school was probably more than a little distressing, okay probably terrifying. For any teachers out there, please don't start an out-of-the-blue phone conversation with "She's okay." It only leads to the worst possible thought in a mother's mind. Anyway, I was insistent about not wanting to go home and for her to bring the plates.

It seemed like only a few short minutes between meeting Mr. Heimlich and my mother finding Becky, my aide at the time, and myself in the bathroom trying to repair the damage the candy and Mr. Heimlich had inflicted. Becky was still shook up, much more than me. I, on the other hand, was more surprised and in awe by the reaction of the "big tough boys" in class, because you know at that age the boys are all big and tough. They cried. I was just happy I didn't have to go home. Btw, hard candy is on my "no go" list with other foods like thick coconut, lettuce, or any raw, hard to chew vegetables, maybe that's why the smoked butterscotch latte at Starbucks is my go to drink when I go there to write, which is most every day.

I've already mentioned that I write children's books. I actually have six under my belt, most of which have a disability element to them. Why, you may ask, did I choose to do so? Because while I was growing up my parents could only find two books with disabled characters in them, neither of which had a worthwhile storyline, nor did they have positive or realistic representations of people with disabilities. There were no disabled characters portrayed as positive role models.

Basically, for as long as I can remember I have always wanted to write books, books with characters that kids with disabilities could assimilate with, just like any other able-bodied kid has the ability to do. When I was a small child I wanted to read about kids like me, and there just weren't any. I kind of always wanted to fix what I thought was a problem, but I didn't really know how to go about something like that, so the idea lay dormant for quite a few years, that is until I rolled into Mrs. Kennedy's eighth-grade English class.

Mrs. Kennedy reignited my desire to write books, books with not only disabled characters, but books that had disabled characters with strong, positive role models as the protagonist. She was one of those teachers that seemed to have the gift of rooting out each of her students' interests and strengths and push them towards their goals. I didn't know it at the time, but this was going to be one of my grown-up goals. Yes, a goal that even a physically disabled, wheelchair bound person could achieve.

This is my first venture outside of the genre of children's books, a venture long overdue. I say long overdue because over the years my family and I have been asked a barrage of questions about my life, how I live it, how others live it with me, and have been or included themselves in my life. Hopefully, I have addressed some of those topics and answered some of those questions within the pages of this book.

But I have to warn you, if you read this book, my story, expecting to find all of the answers to all of your questions, I'm sorry, because disabled or not, we each have our own different, truly, unique story. If help, ideas, inspiration or just a good read was what you were looking for, I hope I've provided that for you. What I'm saying is what worked for me might not work for you, but be creative, try everything, find what works for you, your child, your situation and go with it.

Something I seemed to have forgotten to mention is the importance of becoming your child's advocate, and teaching him or her to do the same for themselves. When I was four years old my dad taught me that very lesson. Besides being an avid bicyclist, he was and is also an avid reader, a love he instilled in me by way of our weekly library trips. The only detouring problem was the fact that there were no designated handicapped parking spaces anywhere near the library.

Long story short, my dad and I went to the city council meeting with our complaint and asked why that was the case and requested the change be made, the issue corrected. That night all things seemed to line up with the stars. Remember Peggy, my aide? Her husband happened to work for the local newspaper and was also present at the meeting...with pen and camera in hand, mind you. I have to tell you, having "the cute factor" and knowing the right people worked in my favor, big time! The article he wrote made front page, above the fold, and the next week a blue parking space had been placed right in front of the library.

If the stars line up or not, align and surround yourself with open-minded people who will support and believe in all possibilities. Don't try and do this alone. Seek out and find any and all resources that are available to you. There are all kinds of state and federal organizations, and even some as close as county, that are in place to help not only financially, but emotionally and physically as well, and know that you have the right to use them. And most importantly...have a sense of humor. Life is too hard without it.

Oh, and define and "Be Your Own Diva," and then own it!

Little Bits About Me...

Born February 18, 1980, at 3:14 a.m., weighing in at 1710 gm or 3 lbs. 12 oz. and topping out at 42 cm or 16.1/2 in. long.

My homecoming-Five weeks from my birth- sometime in March

Baptized twice. Once in the hospital should I have not lived, and then again in 1983, with the appropriate PARTY.

First eight-hour night of sleep- May 23, 1980

First roll over-May 18, 1980

First laugh-November 22, 1980 (I guess it took me a while to develop my sense of humor. Good things are worth waiting for, I guess.)

First tooth- December 30, 1980

First word-Daddy

First phrase-I'm good!

First favorite thing-books (some things never change...still my favorite thing)

First made up saying-gee-gee (I don't remember exactly what it meant, but I thought it was hysterical.)

Diva or not so Diva?!

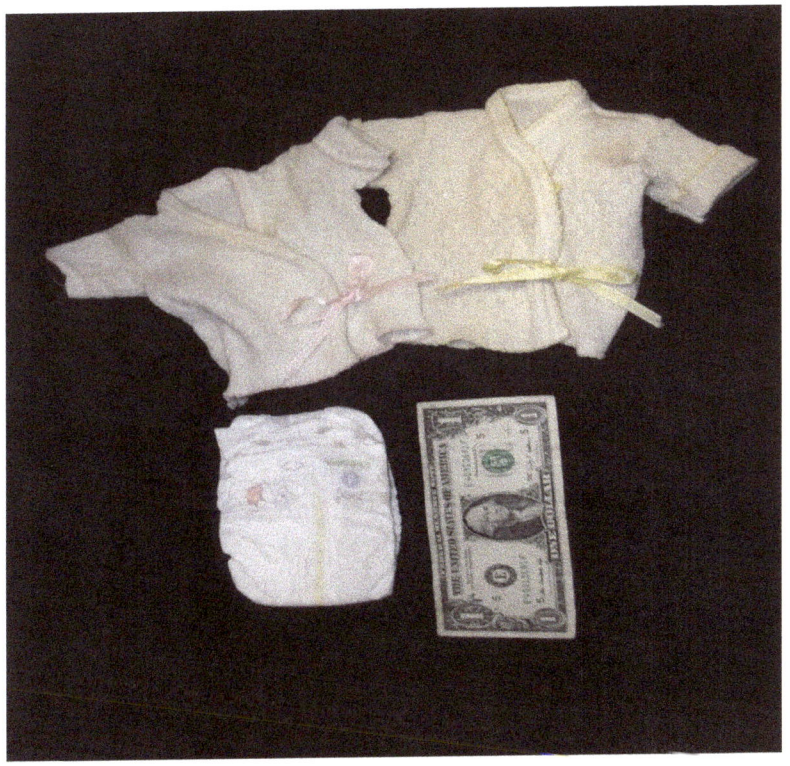

This is what was considered fashionable in the Neonatal Intensive Care Unit (NICU) for preemie babies in the 1980s.

My first dress...a doll dress, but it worked.

One type of the infamous and somewhat embarrassing bibs.

Me, Mom, and Weezy on my first Christmas.

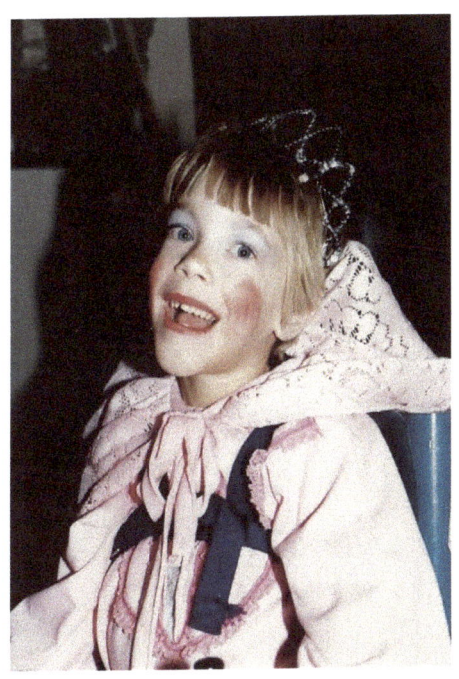

Pink Princess with Full H strap harness pre pierced ears.

Post pierced ears with "H" strap harness totally removed. challenges accepted and smashed.

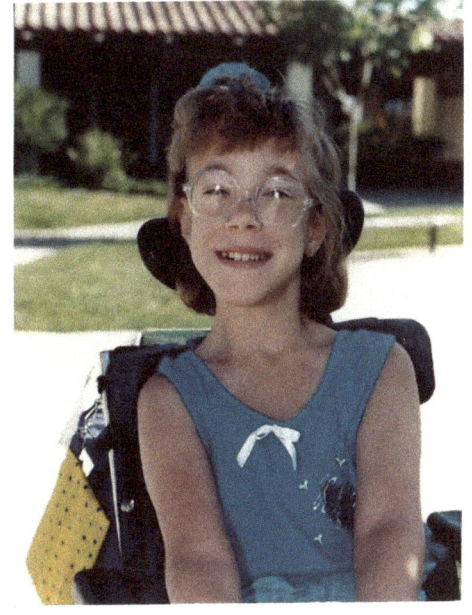

Some of my Besties

Me and my friend, Janice.

Jennifer Kuhns

The Garage Gang

Me and another friend, the orange chair, a wheelchair, highchair, and car seat, which also fit in the bicycle trailer-
One of my other rides.

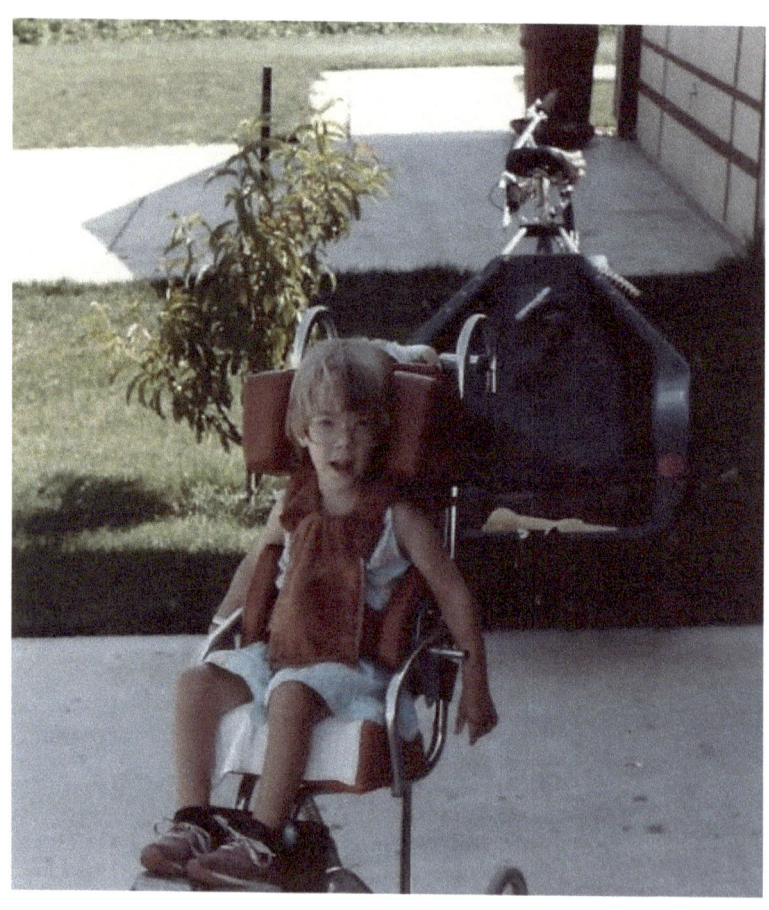

Andrew, my class buddy, and I, collaborating on our science fair project.

Matt, my afterschool buddy, mentor and trouble making partner.

Jennifer Kuhns

All those extracurricular activities my parents let me attempt, succeed or fail.

Showing sheep

4-H demonstrations and public speaking

Jennifer Kuhns

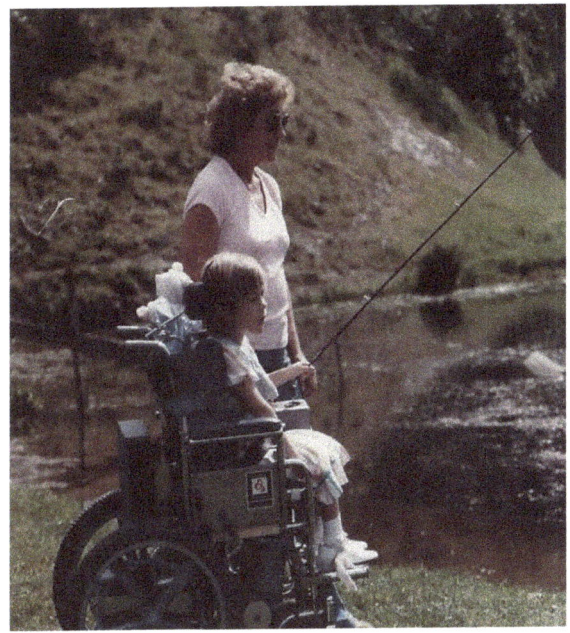

Camping, biking and fishing

Riding and showing horses

Jennifer Kuhns

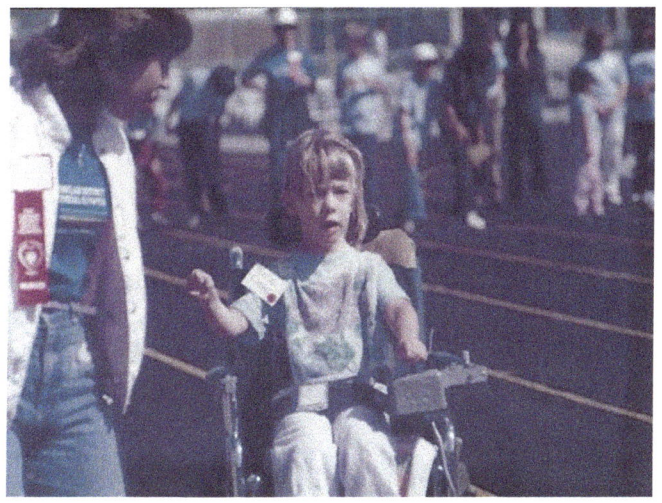

Special Olympics

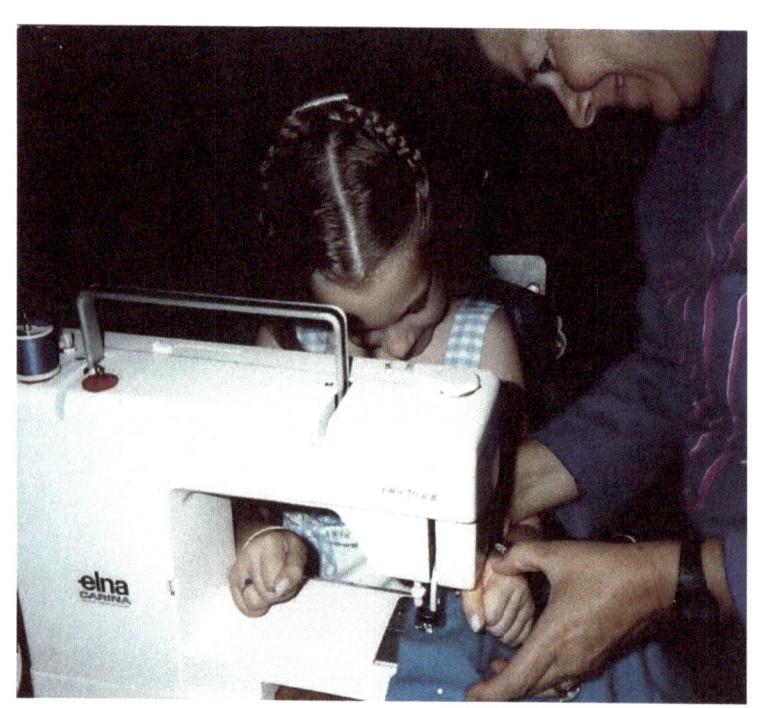

And yes, even sewing!

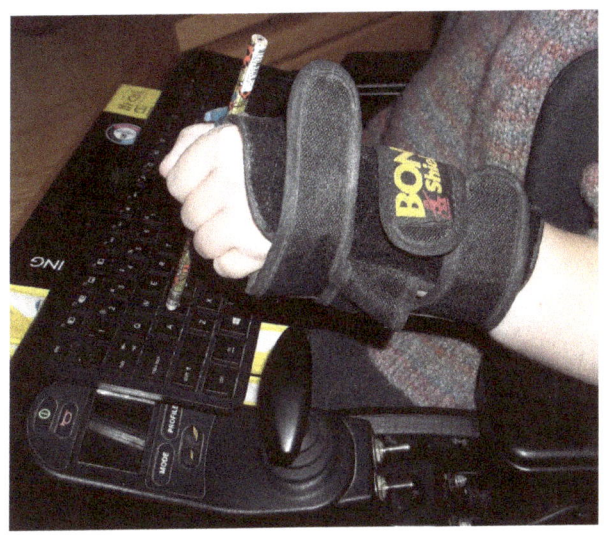

Modern ingenuity
of the time.
My skate boarding
wrist guard with
a pencil attached.

Last, but far from least, my first friends, my fiercest protectors, and greatest supporters, my siblings and my cousins.

My mother's story of my walking soul

I've opted to include this short little story, not necessarily about me, but more about one of my mother's experiences. I've talked about my orange Naugahyde wheelchair, the one that was a wheelchair, highchair, and car seat. It pretty much did everything but allow me to get around by myself, and that seemed to be some kind of a subconscious issue for me. Let me explain. As the story goes:

One night after putting me to bed with Weezy and my pacifier, my mom settled into her night time chores. She and I were home alone because my dad was working one of his normal sixteen-hour shifts.

That particular night she had decided to make jam with blackberries we had picked the day before. I say "we" picked when I really mean "she" picked, but I was there.

Then my mom goes on to share that with the task of jam making complete, she proceeded to wash the dishes, the pots and the pans from dinner and jam making. As she was deep in thought about nothing, she says she had a "prickly hair on your neck" feeling that someone was watching her. Now, remember only she and I were home and it was nowhere near time for my dad to be coming home yet.

When telling the story, Mom always reenacts her movement, her turning around, looking over her shoulder and seeing me walking around the corner of the hallway wall. Keep in mind here that I don't walk...wheelchair and all that.

You'd think that when she finally told someone about her experience, and it took her several years to do so because she figured people would think she was half a bubble off, she would have said that she had just imagined it, but she was and has always been certain it was...are you ready for this....my soul moving, walking on its own because my wakeful body could not. Weird, right? Interestingly enough, the therapist, one of my therapists not hers, said that that was not an uncommon occurrence, people seeing spirits of the living.

That isn't the strangest part of the story, the thinking you see something you could not have. The strangest part is Mom initially not questioning what she saw as being real, seeing me in the same pajamas I was wearing that night in bed. Not only that, but she insists that I was not walking with a "normal" gate, but with a scissor like gate that is common among people with Cerebral Palsy that have the ability walk to some degree.

The story ends with Mom hustling down the hallway to scold me for being out of bed. It wasn't until she got to my room and saw me lying there, sounder asleep than she had ever seen me, did she suddenly realize that there was no way what she just saw could have ever happened. As she stood dumbfounded by the side of my bed watching me snore softly, to say the least, she was a little freaked out by the whole thing. That is after she came to her senses. Although, to this day she insists she saw what she saw. And I for one am not going to be the one to question when it comes to my mom and a mother's...what should I call it....insight and intuition.

Articles, reviews and reflections

Quicke, John. Disability in Modern Children's Fiction. Cambridge: Brookline, 1985.

This is a very black and white book written about children with disabilities and their fight for acceptance in society. Throughout the presentation of a number of books, themes, and stereotypes, the author, John Quicke, explains exactly what folklore can and does do for children. He understands and brings to the forefront the idea that the topic of disabilities has been tainted by the cultural, historical and societal knowledge or biases of any given time. Common knowledge suggests that "one's response to [literature] inevitably reflects one's personal background, training and current intellectual and emotional concerns" (11). This is where folklore can change the perception of the disabled early in the formative years of a child's educational experience,

Quicke presents a number of works that have been written in the area of children's literature concerning itself with disabilities. At the same time he also expresses the unsettling concept that these writings tend to reinforce the negative attitudes that adults, more often than not, associate with not just disabilities, but being different. Conformity to set social and cultural standards or expectations is high on the acceptability list for adults.

Discrimination plays a large role in how disabled people are characterized in everyday life.

They are either evil, the children of the devil or sacred beings, both of which lack human qualities. This perception is rooted deep within the social and historical representation of disabled people in literature only to be preserved by the parents and/or caregivers of peers. Until children are presented with alternative stereotypes of the disabled this is not likely to change.

Quicke's concern is the need for integration of more progressive and positive ideals of society, primarily in the area of the disabled. He points out that any reading curriculum in the mid nineteen-eighties was based upon the books and authors that portrayed a disabled main character as someone to be pitied or to inspire others. These books deliver the message that disabled people are an inferior group of folks. This mindset needs to be ,and can be, changed through a change in text being written and used in schools.

The research conducted by Quicke prior to nineteen-eighty-five on published children's books concerning or broaching the subject of disabilities found that these books were not very good. Granted, disability is a sensitive topic and because of that sensitivity, he discovered that "most of the books were of poor quality [because] reviewers tend to be too kind to authors who include disabled characters in their stories" (6). Quicke also seemed to have an epiphany himself. Does not the study of literature that opens the door to disabilities in fact categorize and separate them out into a separate group, a different group of folks, a folk group?

It is a cultural and social normalcy to separate out, discriminate against, label and categorize the disabled. They are a "disruptive influence" (38), a burden and animalistic in nature. The books Quicke references in this study up holds the aforementioned belief. Mary Anne, the disabled main character in *The View Beyond My Father* by M.E. Allen, tells her friend: "They think of me as a child and children aren't people [...]" (39-40). Just as discriminatory if not more in text, is the book by Alan Marshall, *I Can Jump Puddles*. The child that this story portrays is a disabled male who has a mother who wants to baby him and a father who dominates every conversation. This author injects into his children's books and reinforces a multitude of accepted beliefs; the most poignant –equality of social standing. In other words, a disabled, black woman (even lower, female child) is considered to be in the lowest social class. The man child in this book, opposed to Mary Anne in *The View Beyond My Father*, is forced to put on a strong front, told that he should take charge and act as part of the higher social class. Although "the bravery stereotype was particularly annoying" (56), Quicke also uncovers in children's literature other oppressive behavior and attitudes portrayed. These are the ideals that are being integrated into the themes and influencing up coming generations of children. *Disability in Modern Children's Fiction* addresses not only the struggle of acceptance by the 'handicapped' person, but the struggle of all groups; race, gender, religious, etc., into the patriarchal society as embodied in children's literature.

    Another aspect that children's literature is attempting to do is convince disabled children to accept things for what they are. Most children's books influence, guide and instruct children to strive for more, for success, to push themselves, to be the best. Children's books that are written for and about disabled children convey an opposite message. As in the book *If Only I Could Walk,* Penny is told by her sister to "face [her] handicap and how it will limit [her]" (119). And in the end Penny accepts that rendition of herself instead of challenging it.

Chapter nine presents Quicke's take on fiction for younger children written specifically about children that are disabled. He has reviewed and commented on several books that have young children depicted as the main character. These books attempt to make a connection between the disabled child and 'normal children'. A connection may in fact be made on a superficial 'I'll be your friend' level. These books are also attempting to influence children by exposing them to factual, situational and educational stories. The first problem he found was that although these books expose children to medical and other scary realities, there is no story line for them to follow. The second problem is that these books employ "vocabulary beyond the reading abilities of most five-year-olds" (135-6). The children may get the gist of the topic from the pictures, but comprehension of the material is questionable at best. A third is the portrayal of the disabled child as unable to do anything a normal child does. Yet another issue that detours children from books on or about disabilities is the poor quality of illustrations. They are generally black and white and more informational looking instead of interesting and stimulating.

In conclusion, Quicke reviews data such as the Hopkins report (1982) that examines "the most recent editions of twelve major basal reading series for references to handicapped individuals [that include] all readers up to the sixth grade" (152). The results were as follows:

Out of 4,656 selections only 39 stories (less than 1 per cent) dealt with any type of handicapping condition. An analysis of 39 stories revealed that (a) there was nothing about handicap before third-grade level; (b) in five of the twelve basal series, stories about handicap occurred in only one of the dozen or more texts in the series, and it was thus possible that a child might be exposed to only one story about a handicapped person in six years at school; (c) blindness was the handicap represented in 25 of the 39 stories; (d) all other handicaps were represented by eight selections. (152)

Quicke believes that there is a need for change in what we are giving children to read, not only in quantity but in quality. He has also determined that children's books should "avoid reinforcing [...] divisions in society in a way which is counterproductive as far as children with disabilities is concerned" (153).

Reflection:
Disability in Modern Children's Fiction

In my opinion the author of *Disability in Modern Children's Fiction*, John Quicke, has penetrated the eye of the storm when it comes to children's literature and the representation and discussion of disabilities. This guy has an absolute handle on the how disabled people are portrayed in and throughout literature. As a disabled person I have lived what Quicke is reporting. When I was growing up my parents searched endlessly for children's books that had a disabled child in them. It was their hope to help me identify with these characters in a positive light. Not only did they find their search exhausting and fairly fruitless (they found a total of two), the characters were classified as "special' from the get go.

Quicke's belief is also my belief. That belief is that as adults, as educators of children, we need to re-evaluate how we characterize not only people with disabilities, but people who are different. But in order to do that, adults must change their own perceptions of the disabled. More importantly, the authors and publishers of children's books need to look at how they are influencing the children of today by looking at what they print and how those children are going to influence the children of tomorrow. One of the first views of the world a child has is through the magical world of literature in which they learn about their past, their future, themselves. Children develop and learn by way of example, be it action or word.

One example comes to mind when I think about how adults influence adults who influence children. Maria Shriver, the first lady of California and news woman has written a book titled, *What's Wrong With Timmy?* Because she is an individual with somewhat of a celebrity status, her book was well received and highly praised. Also as is generally the case, authors who use disabled characters in their stories are given major Kudos. It makes no difference if the story is good or bad. In this particular case, as is too often true, the story does nothing more than demean and has the reader feel sorry for Timmy. Granted the book explains the disability, but it does not challenge it. The book does not portray Timmy as anything more than a pet dog that needs to be fed, bathed and taken for a walk. A similar idea is illustrated in a movie titled The *Mighty* that was adapted from the novel *Freak, The Mighty* in which one of the themes suggests that it takes the two disabled people to create one whole and normal person.

Another one of my fundamental objections to the way and the extent disabilities are represented in children's literature is that the reality of life is that we all have some sort of disability to overcome. The only difference is the degree of the disability. Some are seen some are not. Some are as large as wheelchairs and some are as small as having to wear glasses or having feet that are too big. I find it highly offensive that disabled children, as Quicke points out, are lumped together ....oh wait...I have to step back here and restate what it is I was going to say. ...are lumped together in a group of people ...a group of young folks that are joined by and share circumstances, a way of life as a culture. Excuse me, what better way to describe a folk group. This some may feel pushes the outer edges of the definition of folklore studies, but the fact that disabilities are an issue at all secures them a place in history. By establishing 'having a disability' as a social group opens the door for some realistic discussion of the group.

Books read by children influence, mold and frame their opinions, their way of looking at the world. When they are given the stories that are presently out there, they are left with prejudicial outlooks on the disabled, and don't even give me my soapbox that allows me to address the issues of women and race in literature. They are left with the idea that disabled people are less than whole and deserve less than an equality of rights. Children being what they are, are easily influenced. Disabled children as well as 'normal' children that read and know they are reading fictional stories still tend to believe in them. The opposing messages that are being sent reinforce the separateness and segregation of these two groups of children. Disabled children are given no hope of leaving their disadvantages, their deficiencies behind them while 'normal, able-bodied' children are given the slingshot to shoot for the moon. As an example, I particularly find *I Use a Wheelchair,* a book mentioned by Quicke in his study, especially offensive. Even the pictures show a special school for wheelchair students with no indication that there is any other option for these students.

The one thing that I must give credit for is the real and informational knowledge that some of these books contain. Not all of them nowadays are bad. They show children what disabilities are, but there is a flip side to this. Are we introducing them too late in their educational experience to dissuade negative attitudes? Are we stimulating their interest in the topic with stimulating illustrations as we do with other books? Quicke believes not. I tend to agree.

Holmes, Martha Stoddard. <u>Fictions of Afflictions: Physical Disability in Victorian Culture.</u> Michigan: U of Michigan, 2004.

Fictions of Afflictions is part of a series of books on disability. This particular book is written by Martha Stoddard Holmes, once a professor at Plymouth State and Cal State San Marcos. She also gained insight and help from her students and colleagues who were also interested in Victorian fiction and the representation and portrayal of people with disabilities. Holmes wrote this book to try and answer her own "questions about bodies, emotions, and representations, and how we learn to feel about bodily variation in others and ourselves" (vii). A good portion of her information was gathered through her students' own feelings and assumptions about disability and people with disabilities. It was a difficult subject to broach, but Holmes took her students to the "unimagined territory [,...] to disavow full participation in the identity—'disabled person'" (viii). She says that she knew this would be uncomfortable for them, but also felt the need to uncover and expose the imaginative impasse [that] was a product of those dominant cultural narratives—fictional and otherwise—that teach us what embodiment means, when it is desirable and when it is fearful. When these narratives speak at all about disability, they teach us that it is alien, terrifying, tragic; that it transforms your life in overwhelming negative ways and it is normal to feel horrified, relieved, and inspired, all from a safe distance, when we encounter disability. There are so few other [feelings] suggested by the textual and visual narratives than train us how to picture, talk about, and enact the relationship to our own and others' bodies shaped by the able-disabled binary. (ix)

Within the pages of this book Holmes reveals the representation and feelings felt about the disabled and how they are depicted in Victorian culture through melodramatic examples, both written and performed. The use of disabled characters evokes a certain kind of emotion that was particularly useful in the Victorian era. It was a way to move the audience, for entertainment's sake, past the person with the disability to the significance they portrayed; the disabled woman who could not marry, but could bear children (reproduction was highly important during that time), the poor, blind, orphan boy, Tiny Tim who used a crutch and could die at any moment but instead lived and melted Scrooge's cold heart of stone. In other words, using the image of disability in Victorian literature and theater has influenced the attitudes toward disabilities "to a particular set of emotional codes and to permanently associate the experiences of disability" (4) with inferiority.

Holmes believes facts uphold the idea that "we are all affected by [the] cultural representation of disability" (xi). Each chapter in this book provides an example and/or explanation about the use and thoughts on people with disabilities. Holmes explicitly states that she has no interest in the 'feelings' that people have toward disabilities; the I feel sorry for them, the I am inspired by them, the I don't know what I would do if I were them. She is more interested in how and why disabled people are portrayed in Victorian melodramas, finding that the disabled character seems to represent not a specific character, but a variety of conditions such as helplessness, otherness, "extreme moral and emotional conditions [that work ...] as a metaphor for situations of the working class" (24-5). It was more of a visual experience that provided a model of what was expected of a disabled person. Holmes also relates that the Victorian melodrama was more concerned about ability and disability as an interaction, whereas later, a hundred years or so, disability began to represent social status. Different than Victorian times, disability became more of a topic than an avenue to deliver a message. There "literary works [became] a major vehicle for the transfer of cultural values about disability" (32). The historian Douglas Baynton is referred to by Holmes as is his statement that "disability is everywhere in history, once you begin to look for it" (12). More often than not disability is an easy subject to pigeonhole into a stereotype, a trope used since the Victorian era to represent neediness, invisibility and is somewhere on the other side of patriarchal society, but more invisible than women, African Americans, Native Americans, homosexuals, etc.

Holmes has found through her studies that disability occurs and reoccurs in a considerable amount of literature and mentions them by name in this book. She presents the association of disability with women, for example, in The Last Days of Pompeii, The Cricket on the Hearth, Olive, The Clever Women of the Family, and Our Mutual Friend as a change begins to take place allowing disabled women to participate in life. She denotes that Victorian narratives had a hard time incorporating disabled women into societal roles as wives, mothers or sexual partners, but had depended on "emotional excess" to create drama in the stories or tales. This was especially true for women who were shown to suffer and who learned to live with their disability, to think of it as a blessing of sorts because it allowed them not to have to endure the marriage bed. It is seen "that the construct [ion of] disabled women as emotionally excessive women and explicitly mark them as unfit for marriage" (56). Sally Mitchell, critic and professor of Women's Studies at Temple University, suggests that the representation of disabled women differed between male and female authors in Victorian literature. Women writers, she says, reproduce the thoughts and feelings of women, "the pain of helplessness, the lack of power and social position and financial ability and legal right to control the circumstances of one's own life (Dinah Mulock Craik 112)" (60), thus creating an outlet and avenue for change. The shift in thinking connects disabled women to normalcy, for example, the likeness of disabled women to able women in the need for emotional and sexual love, its existence and "centrality to humanness itself" (73).

Women and disability are entwined with sexual behavior, desire and performance. What are the historical views of men? The male figure that is disabled has been reduced to female confines or else become beggars. Either way, they are unable to earn money and support a family. Probably the most well-known disabled male character is Tiny Tim in A Christmas Carol by Dickens. Year after year the world re-visits Tiny Tim and cries for the poor 'crippled' boy. And then we cry again when he is cured of his affliction, and we can imagine the wonderful life he now has in front of him. This reincarnation of the stereotypical male figure releases Tiny Tim from the life promised to him, that of disabled men "a host of terrifying, leering old men with avarice, deception and smoggy sexuality hovering about them [...] who bilk money from good people; ogle, stalk and knock down little girls; and terrify young boys" (95).

Like disabled women in Victorian melodramas, disabled men are represented and reoccur. The male figure, however, seems to have no middle ground. He is either an "innocent afflicted child [... or] wicked man [because] the disabled worker" (96) has no melodramatic pull. Disabled boys induce a certain amount or degree of 'excess' and like women and girls remain on the outside of society. Disabled boys, which differ from disabled females, "produce emotional growth and connection to others" (99), and are "honestly deserving" (100).

So, now what defines deserving and deserving what? Even in Victorian times disabled children were classified or categorized and determined if they were or were not eligible for aid. What happens to those children who are of a social status or standing that eradicates them from such services? In real Victorian life "The afflicted child was any[one] incapacitated and dependent [and]deserves pity, tenderness, and financial support and a duplicitous, avaricious, and probably malingering beggar is blatantly undeserving of any of these" (100). In so many words there was a literature imitating life scenario that anchored and stabilized the shifting economy of emotions that characterized discussions of physical disability. In theory [...] all disabled people [are judged by] nondisabled people as [either] innocently dependent [or...] guiltily dependent, despite the fact that their feelings toward all disabled people (and all dependent people) were probably mixed. [...] While afflicted children are predictably more common to educational texts, and beggars are indigenous to the writings of social reformers, the figure of the beggar shadows educational text as a probable fate of graduates of schools for blind or deaf people, given public resistance to employing people with disabilities. (100-101)

Some children may have been given the title of deserving but none of the disabled characters in history, in word or life have been given value. Holmes isn't saying that they are un- educable although the idea was questioned. In fact, education of the disabled, especially the deaf and blind, has been used as an educational tool itself. As explained, educating the disabled is a 'feel good' point. It makes society feel good that it is paying attention to those in need and less fortunate and transforming through learning "these poor neglected little ones into busy happy pupils" (103). Again the author shows the underlying reality of thought about disability. These students, the blind for example, may be taught Braille, but they are never taught or guided into a profession, craft or trade. They have nothing more than *heartfelt* sympathy and with the "emotional constructions of impairment so deeply woven into Victorian culture, the real problems with vocational training for disabled people were most likely perceptual and attitudinal rather than logistical" (107) as previously mentioned. It is these beliefs that caused and still cause poor quality of educational programs for the disabled. In addition the representation of the disabled is not only present in melodramas, but also in educational writings and policies as well as social culture.

Up until this point Holmes relates what people other than disabled people thought, felt, believed, about disabled people in the nineteenth century. Surprisingly (or not), disabled people have been influenced in their own existence by cultural and social realms. In the remaining chapters Holmes unleashes the disabled on themselves as they uphold the same attitudes about their lives and "habitually locate themselves in relation to melodramatic figurations of disability" (135). Through these biographies and autobiographies the disabled person finds him/herself caught between misery and hope.

From <u>London Labour and the London Poor</u>, the crippled street seller of Nutmeg-graters takes on the persona of the humble and accepting disabled lot in life. He relates his tear-jerking story of being the illegitimate disabled child of an unmarried woman who pays someone else to care for him when she does marry. Then she all but abandons him in some type of school and visits once a year. The street seller's recollection is upbeat and high spirited, saying that "no mother couldn't have loved a child more than mine did" (138). Later in the interview the melancholy nuance of despair becomes apparent as the street seller tells of his contemplation of suicide.

When I've gone along the streets, too, and been in pain, I've thought, as I've seen the people pass straight up, with all the use of their limbs, and some of them the biggest blackguards, cussing and swearing, I've thought, Why should I be deprived of the use of mine? [A]nd I felt angry like, and perhaps at that moment I couldn't bring my mind to believe the Almighty was so good and merciful as I'd heard say; but then in a minute or two afterwards I've prayed to Him to make me better and happier in the next world. I've always been led to think He's afflicted me as He has for some wise purpose or another that I can't see. I think as mine is so hard a life in this world, I shall be better off in the next (1:330-31). (138)

Disabled writers themselves bounce between the melodramatic stereotype that culture and society has placed them in and a more truthful representation of what the disabled desire. Holmes found that the "middle –class people [she] discusses devoted much of their lives to reestablishing disability in material, not emotional terms advocating for better training and employment, disseminating practical information to other disabled people" (149). Harriet Martineau (1802-1876), one of the nineteenth century's prominent (disabled) writers addresses the myths about the care of and for the disabled in a speech:

We must destroy the sacredness of the subject, by speaking of it ourselves: not perpetually and sentimentally, but, when occasion rises, boldly, cheerfully, and as a plain matter of fact. When everybody about us gets to treat it as a matter of fact, our daily difficulties are almost gone; and when we have to do with strangers, the simple, cheerful declaration, "I am very deaf," removes almost all trouble. (152)

Martineau continues with such statements as "tenderness is hurtful to us in as far as it encourages us to evade our enemy" (152) and not facing them head on, and "under a bondage of self-denial, which annihilates [...] all the pleasure [...], we must bravely go on taking our place in society" (152). So even though she stands, fights and gains credibility for disabled people she falls prey to the trappings of struggle and resignation. She accepts, full faced, defeat and denial. Martineau gains power for disability only to give it back to the long standing cultural ruling.

There is no question that literature moves cultural, social and historical values and trends about disabilities from the nineteenth century to modern times. The question that does arise for this author is how and why disability affected and saturated Victorian fiction. She also wonders how contemporary literature already consumed by "meanings of work, class and gender [will shuffle in complicated] cultural constructions of disability" (186). If nothing else it will cause us to become aware of the assumptions and misconceptions about cultural values in relation to disability.

Reflection:
Fictions of Afflictions: Physical Disability in Victorian Culture

Martha Stoddard Holmes and her curiosity about people and disability prompted her to write <u>Fictions of Afflictions: Physical Disability in Victorian Culture.</u> By revisiting through literature the Victorian era, Holmes has exposed maybe not the origin, but at least the beginnings of misunderstanding and tainted assumptions about disability and the people it affects. I am really pleased with Holmes' interest in the thoughts about and feelings towards people with disabilities. Before something, an attitude, belief, ritual, custom, or whatever can be changed or altered it must be dissected, studied and understood. Holmes investigates the matter beyond the two annoyingly, pacifying or demeaning remarks that I am constantly bombarded with; "You are such an inspiration" or with a pat on the head, "You poor thing, you are so special."

I wish I could have seen her class plunged into "full participation in the identity" (viii), especially since the men in her class were, as she observed, "detached, guilty, irritated, and anxious" (viii) when talking about not only disabilities, but about feelings in general. It has always been my experience that the things we are most afraid of are the things we try to remove from our world or belittle to the point of non-existence. Since the world is basically male dominated, patriarchal in nature, it doesn't surprise me in the least that the males in Holmes' class would react this way, nor does it surprise me that the women in the class would talk about and felt comfortable talking about anything except disabilities. I can also understand why people with disabilities were used in Victorian melodramas. What is more entertaining than having your heartstrings pulled? I can just see the frustration and disbelief in the eyes of her students as they delve into disability and its portrayal and face their fears.

A fact that is quite interesting to me is that there has indeed been a cultural change in belief and treatment of those that are disabled, it has gotten worse. In the melodramas of the Victorian era, disability was used as a trope for the "haves" and "have nots." During this time disabled people were illustrated as being needy and non-disabled people were shown as the ones to fill the need. Tiny Tim was mentioned numerous times in connection with his neediness, his family's neediness. When the cultural change takes place it is then understood that Tiny Tim is crippled as some kind of punishment for his family being poor. He is later cured by some kind of miracle and God's will. Yeah, that is a little scary how the same story can be maneuvered and manipulated to exemplify that cultural change, the move to have disability embody social status.

After this shift it is not a reach to assume that women would be the next target or tool in Victorian literature. Women are, of course, lower than a rock in any social or cultural hierarchy. Slap a disability on them and they are still under a rock but they are shown to struggle with passion against suffering (whatever they are suffering from, which can be because of what they don't have or what they do have, and generally it has something to do with sex) and then compelled to not only accept their dilemma, but be happy for it. An interesting fact became evident to me as well. Disabled women are unfixable and must live within the confines of their disability. Boys, on the other hand, like Tiny Tim are fixable. Why is this? Well my guess would be that since most of the authors are men, they write what they believe to be true, or think should be true, developing a stereotype. Some critics discuss this theory as being a "detour from reality [while others see] them for being too real" (90). Either way disabled boys are only fixable if they are of the proper social class. If they are not fixable they are financially supported and all other needs are taken care of, but are considered somewhat feminine, displaying "emotional growth and connection [to] others, while always remaining outside the world of adulthood and homosocial and other bonds based on equality" (99). Otherwise the disabled boys become lowly, good for nothing beggars and child molesters.

Another topic that I have had much experience with it that of education. Since it is the non-disabled people that make decisions for the disabled concerning their capability you would think that the aforementioned would have a certain amount of, I don't know—practical or common or inside knowledge as to the cognitive level of disabled students. A non-disabled five-year-old and a non-disabled ten-year-old do not function on the same level, why should disabled ones. I absolutely have seen the "feel good" education plan in action. When I began my educational career in special education pre-school I was taught how to brush my teeth, to wait my turn, to clean my plate, and any other accepted behavioral patterns. The difference between myself and other members of the class is that I was physically disabled and some of them were mentally disabled. They were kept happy and busy while the teachers pushed me a little harder. They tested my memory, for example by teaching me little rhymes like "Pink, pink, you stink" and Blue, blue, shame on you." I actually remember one aide saying that I was fun because I had a brain that actually worked and could remember. But that was pre-school where kids are taught how to put on their shoes and not taught to think.

This particular cultural belief and practice has not changed much since the Victorian era. It is still believed that anything more than life skills need not be taught to disabled children. It is believed that it is a waste of time to educate disabled people. I have had to fight the system for a place in the classrooms of higher education as well as in the minds of the educators. At this point in time I am pursuing my Master's Degree and yet must defend the idea that I have a professional goal in mind. Granted, it is a stereotypical profession for a disabled person as an author, and it may be regarded as a cop out or that I am falling prey to the social and cultural confines, but my aim is to change through writing about disabilities the view of people with disabilities by pulling from my own experiences. I can present to children, my chosen audience, non-disabled people's views as well as the views and feelings of disabled people. My plan is not to "habitually locate [myself] in relation to melodramatic figurations of disability" (135), but to remove from the concourse of literature, children's literature specifically, the melodramatic figure of disability.

In reading the autobiographies of disabled people I find it quite annoying that the only two options they believe themselves to have is either suicide or "bravely go on taking our place in society" (152). This really pissed me off and made me stop and think. Yes, I need assistance in life, but we all do in some way or another. I just need more. I understand that being disabled, in a wheelchair in my case, is an oddity but it doesn't make me stupid, blind, deaf and immoral in character. My parents have always allowed me, challenged me to try all kinds of different things, experience all the experiences that I can, "normal" (Normal is such a relative word.) or otherwise. I consider myself equally deserving of...everything that non-disabled people are deserving of. But, since I need more am I asking for too much?

In spite of all that I just said I do retain a certain degree of comradery with the disabled people of the Victorian era I just talked about. My question now is; am I too backing up into the safe sanctity of resignation? Do I really believe that I am asking for too much and am undeserving, or is that just what I have been taught?

***

Other Books by This Author

Were You Born In That Chair?

A Box Full Of Letters

Hailey's Dream

Paisley Or Plaid

Looking For Lola/Taco

Miles To The Moon

Available at your favorite bookstore or at:
www.shalakopress/books.com

www.ingramcontent.com/pod-product-compliance
Lightning Source LLC
Chambersburg PA
CBHW051548010526
44118CB00022B/2626